Take A Second Look

Noel Kirkpatrick

Author of In the Shadow of the Gantries

ALKON PRESS
68 Belfast Road
COMBER
Newtownards
Co Down
BT23 5QP

Published by Alkon Press
Typeset by Hallographics, Belfast.
Printed by Romac Ltd., Belfast.

All photographs of
THE ARDS TT RACES
are by courtesy of
The Ulster Folk & Transport Museum, Cultra.

Front cover design: Ray Wilson
Back cover photograph: Donna Broderick
Graphic sketches: Dr Janice Bailie

ISBN 0 9520190 1 9

TO THE MEMORY OF MY PARENTS
ANDREW (ANDY) AND ELLEN (NELLIE)
KIRKPATRICK OF WHOM I HAVE
FONDEST AND CHERISHED MEMORIES.

ACKNOWLEDGEMENTS

I would like to express my gratitude to the following people who gave me encouragement and inspiration to put my memories into print. Firstly to my dear wife Rita without whose backing and dedication this publication would not have been possible. To my dear friend Noreen Glover and her daughters Roberta and Jean for all their help and assistance. To Janice Bailie, daughter of Roberta and David and grand-daughter of Noreen, for doing the graphic sketches from my hand drawings, to my friends Betty George, Charlie Ludlow and Rosemary Evans for their encouragment; Ray Wilson for his constructive advice and design of the front cover and other aspects of the book; Doreen McBride, herself a successful writer who started me on the road to self publishing, and Joyce Cairns. To the following who have assisted me with information and/or the loan of photographs — Mrs Yvonne Duncan, Mr Len Ball, Mrs Eva Gamble, Mrs Madge Stevenson, Mr Bertie Frazer, Mr Hugh McWhinney (Butcher) The Square, Mr Hugh Mawhinney (Butcher) Castle Street, Mrs Dorothy Murdoch, Mrs Maureen Lennox, Mr Eddie Doherty, Mr Norman Nevin — Local Historian for allowing me to use extracts from his unpublished records, the Ards Historical Society for history of Ards Hospital, the Wesley Methodist Historical Records Office, Mr Tom Andrews of John Andrews Spinning Mill, Mr Andrew Montgomery of James E McCabe Ltd., for information on Comber Distillery, George Hall of Hallographics for his assistance in the production of the book and Ronnie Anderson of Romac Limited — the printers of the book. Finally the staff of Comber Library for all their help and assistance.

CONTENTS

INTRODUCTION

I was always keen on the outdoor life and followed the pursuits of hill walking, underwater diving, caving and general exploring around the countryside until I had a stroke in 1976. It seemed as if my world had collapsed around me but it was then I found that when one door shuts another opens. Although I was not able to continue with my leisure activities I started putting pen to paper and in November 1992 my first book "IN THE SHADOW OF THE GANTRIES" was published. This book is an insight into my childhood days growing up in East Belfast and later my apprenticeship in Harland & Wolff.

In this my second book "TAKE A SECOND LOOK" I hope to make the reader aware how more things come to prominence after a second look. How many times has a second glance at a scene, a place, a photograph revealed more details missed the first time. I invite the reader in the future to become more curious and to — take a second look!

Chapter 1
COMBER

I have lived in Comber for the past 25 years since my marriage to Rita. It is a little town with such a wealth of history that it would warrant a book on its own. This is only a tip of the iceberg as the book is on a broader theme of County Down. Mr Norman Nevin, local historian and past Headmaster of Comber Primary School, has done a lot of research into Comber's history and produced a documentary folder with photographs and other items of interest which he presented to Comber Library. To complement and add to Mr Nevin's collection, Len Ball for some years now has been recording various aspects of Comber with 'still' and 'cine' cameras. Len is also researching into the existing old photographs and adding

Len Ball with camera on site, 27.2.93.

Len Ball's business card.

relevant and informative text. It is his ambition to expand as much as possible on this project so that the Library will have an even greater wealth of material on Comber for reference purposes. To this end Len is always on the look-out for old photographs, cine films or information on old Comber especially anything on the Comber railway and Ards TT race.

He has facilities for reproducing copies of anything submitted to him so that owners will have their originals returned.

COMBER is situated in the County of Down and along Strangford Lough. Strangford Lough got its name from the Vikings when they visited these shores. It is derived from their interpretation of 'Strong Fjord' because of the strong currents in the lough. COMBER itself was formerly known by different names such as COMMER, CUMBER or 'COMAR'. The latter is an Irish word meaning the joining of two rivers which in this case would refer to the INLER and the GLEN rivers. COMBER is reputed to have been at one time a Stage Coach Centre en route between Belfast and Downpatrick. Of course this would have been before the time of the railways. Quite a few historical events, notable characters and industries have, through the passage of time, put Comber on the map. The Breweries, Flour Milling, Bleaching, Rice Starch Factory and Wisharts Nut and Bolt Factory with others have all gone but the Comber Spinning Mill is operating to this day. Andrews Spinning Mill and McWhinney's Butcher Shop are two of the oldest businesses in the town which retain family links and their descendants still trade, to this day, using the family name.

The Albion Stitching Factory, Castle Lane, in this century has also supplied employment for a large number of people and is still trading to this day.

McWhinney's Butcher Shop — The Square

McWhinney's butcher shop in Comber Square is the oldest trading shop in Comber going back as far as 1892 in its first site in Castle Street. It moved to a different site in Castle Street where Harry Frazer's Chip Shop is now before its present location in Comber Square where it has been since the 1920s. It was the custom then for the shop to be "dressed up" outside every Christmas for a few days as shown in the photograph. It was on these occasions that a man and a dog were used to guard the meats on display outside the shop. The present Hugh McWhinney who now runs the shop is the grandson of the Hugh McWhinney in the photograph.

Sir Rollo Gillespie

Major General Sir Rollo Gillespie, K.C.B., was born in Comber and his famous last words of 'ONE SHOT MORE FOR THE HONOUR OF DOWN' as he lay dying at the battlefield of Kalunga in 1814 have made him a household name in Comber and further afield ever since. The very tall and impressive statue which was erected to him still stands in Comber Square and round it are recorded names of various battles. Adjacent to this statue is the War Memorial, erected in 1923, which features the figure of a soldier and records the names of those in the town and district who died as well as those who served in the First World War 1914-1918.

My wife told me when she was a little girl there was always an amusing incident when a new policeman was posted into the town. It was a common trick for local lads when stopped for having no lights on their bicycles or similar minor offences, to give their name and address as Gillespie, The Square, Comber. Many a poor policeman was taken in by this but was certainly made aware at a very early stage in his new post who Gillespie really was!

McWhinney's butcher shop dressed up for Christmas in the 1920s. Left — Tansey Lee Humphries, centre - Mr. Lundy, right — Hugh McWhinney.

Gillespie Monument, 1900s.

Edmund De Wind VC

A 135 mm German Field Gun used to be positioned in The Square before the present gardens were laid out.

This was in fact presented to the town by the War Office as a tribute to the courage of Second Lieutenant Edmund De Wind, VC, from Comber who served in the 15th Battalion of the Royal Irish Rifles and was mortally wounded in March 1918. He was posthumously awarded the Victoria Cross and his name and details were inscribed on the side of the Field Gun. Sadly the gun fell victim along with garden railings and similar items which all went for scrap

135 quick firing German field gun, 1920s.

metal for the Second World War effort 1939-45. However the metal plates containing the following inscriptions were preserved and can be seen in the porch of St Mary's Parish Church in Comber Square.

TOP TABLET:

THE TABLET IS FROM THE GERMAN GUN FORMERLY IN THE SQUARE AND RECORDS THE DEEDS OF EDMUND DE WIND, 2ND LIEUTENANT, 15TH BATT. ROYAL IRISH RIFLES FOR WHICH HE WAS POSTHUMOUSLY AWARDED THE VICTORIA CROSS.

BOTTOM TABLET:

FOR MOST CONSPICUOUS BRAVERY AND SELF SACRIFICE ON THE 21 MARCH 1918 AT THE RACE COURSE REDOUBT NEAR GROAGIE FOR SEVEN HOURS HE HELD THIS MOST IMPORTANT POST AND THOUGH TWICE WOUNDED AND PRACTICALLY SINGLE-HANDED. HE MAINTAINED HIS POSITION UNTIL ANOTHER SECTION COULD BE GOT TO HIS HELP. ON TWO OCCASIONS WITH TWO NCO's ONLY, HE GOT ON THE TOP UNDER HEAVY MACHINE-GUN AND RIFLE FIRE AND CLEARED THE ENEMY OUT OF THE TRENCH KILLING MANY. HE CONTINUED TO REPEL ATTACK AFTER ATTACK UNTIL HE WAS MORTALLY WOUNDED AND COLLAPSED. HIS VALOUR, SELF-SACRIFICE AND EXAMPLE WERE OF THE HIGHEST ORDER.

A white marble tablet also in the Church Porch records names of parishioners in the First World War under the following inscription:

1914-1919
THE HEROIC DEAD AND THOSE WHO SERVED AND RETURNED

Comber Square showing Gillespie Statue and smaller War Memorial, October 1993.

St Mary's Parish Church

This church is over 300 years old and was built on the site of a former Cistercian Abbey.

Our present Queen when she was Princess Elizabeth visited the church in 1946. The occasion was when she was Godmother at the christening of Elizabeth Lavinia Sarah — baby daughter of Elizabeth Patricia and Osborne King. A photograph recording this event is in the Church Vestry. The baby's mother Elizabeth Patricia was Lady-in-Waiting to Princess Elizabeth.

In the 1970s Rita and I had the privilege of being taken up to the clock tower by Fred Carson who was then the sexton of the church. I had previously mentioned to him about being interested in seeing the mechanism. Fred pointed to the high ceiling

St. Mary's Parish Church, Comber, October 1993.

where I saw a long ladder leading almost up to a trap door which gave access to the flag pole on the roof. Now as heights held no terror for me, I accepted the challenge and opportunity to view the town from the top of the clock tower.

Fred climbed up almost as far as the high ceiling and reaching above displaced the square trap door. Then with a nimble 'about turn' he was half in half outside the tight hole. He swiftly drew himself out unto the belfry roof. He shouted down for me to follow and that was when the fun began. When I reached the top of the vertical ladder I was still several feet below and out of line to the trap door above. I had to turn the wrong way round and grasp the wooden square surround of the hole to draw myself outside. The view from the top was delightful and we spent some time pointing out landmarks. The bell started to clang down below and I thought my wife Rita who had been waiting there, had accidentally moved

Fred Carson as a young man.

Fred Carson in his Sexton's robes.

one of the clock levers, but apparently it was only on the strike.

It was my turn to descend first as Fred had to close the square trap door in the roof. Coming down was even more hair-raising than going up especially as my feet were the wrong way round on the vertical ladder. However we both descended safely to my wife's relief and when I challenged Fred about the mis-match from the ladder to the trap door, he laughed and said — it was to sort out the men from the boys! On returning to the road outside and looking up at the Church Tower it was hard to believe that such a hazard existed in climbing to the top. I was always grateful to Fred for giving me the opportunity of inspecting the clock tower.

Sadly Fred died in 1985 at the age of 86 and a Memorial Service for him was held in the Church on the 28th June 1985. During his time in office as Sexton, Fred lived with his sister Peggy in the little cottage at the back of the Parochial Hall. This has since been demolished and a new bungalow built which was used by former Curates. The Parochial Hall itself was built in 1953 and is at present undergoing extension and renovations including a new kitchen.

Figure of man in white cobblestones, Comber Square, 1991.

'AUREEN', Comber Square — Figures on Cobbled Footpath

On the opposite side of The Square to St Mary's Church and adjacent to the Northern Bank just in front of the historic house named 'AUREEN', is the remains of a very old cobbled footpath with outlines marked out in white cobble stones. Although this part of the footpath is quite damaged and worn the outlines can still be plainly seen of a hare, a dog and a man. Apparently the dog represents the famous greyhound 'Master McGra' who in the late 1800s won the coveted Waterloo Cup for his owner Lord Lurgan beating the best dogs in Britain. The figure of the man represents the dog's trainer.

First Comber Presbyterian Church

This church is situated at the top of High Street. The congregation was established as far back as 1645 and is believed to be one of the oldest in connection with the Irish Presbyterian Church. The church itself was built in the 1670s. The original part of the building was

First Comber Presbyterian Church, September 1993.

towards The Square. It has had a few extensions added on as the congregation increased over the years.

A western gable was built and 50 years later another wing was added giving the building a "T" shape. The last extension was built in 1740 and this gave the church a cruciform shape.

Second Comber Presbyterian Church

The building of this church in Killinchy Street commenced in the early part of 1839 and was finally dedicated in October 1840. It is ideally situated in a prominent site on raised ground with a spacious frontage giving it an air of seclusion and distinction.

Second Comber Presbyterian Church, September 1993.

Comber Distilleries — Old Comber Whiskey

Comber has had a distillery as far back as the mid 1700s or even earlier. This was known as the Mound Distillery because of an earthen mound to the rear of the buildings. The site was in what is now known as Killinchy Street. Later an additional distillery came into being which was known as the Lower Distillery while the 'Mound' became known as the Upper Distillery. In 1827 John Gaffikin ran the Upper Distillery which prospered having developed

The chimney of Comber Distillery, September 1993.

a reputation for fine whiskey. The excellent quality of Old Comber Whiskey is confirmed by the fact that as far back as 1905, over fifty per cent of it was sold in bottles which was unusual at that time as most Irish Whiskey was sold in casks and was used for blending. Later on, the Distillers Company of Scotland bought up quite a few Irish Distilleries including United Distillers which had three distilleries in Belfast, either to remove them as competitors or use their malt whiskies for blending. Incidentally the biggest whiskey producers in the world just after the First World War was Dunvilles of Belfast. Comber Distillery being a specialist producer did not have the financial resources behind it to prosper in the more competitive world emerging after 1945. Also the financial burden to the Company was too great when, in the mid-1940s, a robbery took place on its premises and a large quantity of whiskey was taken out through the roof. In 1953 it was bought over by H & D Wines of Inverness for its stock and closed down. H & D Wines then sold the Company label to James E McCabe, Wholesale Wine & Spirit Merchants of Portadown. During the 1970s and 80s, McCabes gathered up stocks of Comber whiskey, enough to be commercially viable. However, stocks were limited and the last bottling actually occurred in June 1993. This comprised about 5,000 bottles of Old Comber Whiskey which is a minimum of 40 years old.

The Chapel

This chapel 'THE CHURCH OF THE VISITATION OF THE BLESSED VIRGIN MARY' is also in Killinchy Street and is well over a hundred years old. The foundation stone was laid on 23rd October 1868 and the Church, built of stone in early Gothic style, was dedicated in 1872. Sadly it suffered severe damage on 5th January 1993 due to an incendiary device and after repairs and a complete refurbishment was re-dedicated on the 4th July 1993.

The Church of the Visitation of the Blessed Virgin Mary, September 1993.

The Ghost Hole

Continuing on out the Killinchy Road, and just beyond the Riverview Garage is a tidal inlet known as the 'Ghost Hole' 'Gaste Hole' or 'Geest Hole' as it was sometimes called. There are some small boats moored here. I enquired as to how this particular spot was so named and was told that in bygone years there was smuggling activity of spirits, probably brandy at this location. The

The Ghost Hole, 1973.

smugglers, wanting privacy for their activities, had a ghostly apparition placed in the vicinity during the hours of darkness to frighten people away and thus this area became known as the Ghost Hole.

Railway Engine House

Travelling from Dundonald direction along the Comber By-Pass is a slip road to the right called Glen Link which leads onto the junction of Railway Street, Glen Road or into Comber Main Street. On the left hand side just before the junction is the site where the Comber Railway Station used to be.

The station itself was demolished in the early 1950s after the closure of this particular railway line. The halts from Comber to Belfast were COMBER, DUNDONALD, KNOCK, NEILLS HILL, BLOOMFIELD, BELFAST. In the opposite direction the lines went to NEWCASTLE via DOWNPATRICK. The last remaining evidence of the railway system is the actual platform where people used to mount and alight on and off the trains. Also the complete engine

The railway engine house in Comber with 'God Save The King' around the archway, 1991.

house which is still intact, is now used as a car exhaust business. This engine house was formerly used to accommodate a railway steam engine on stand-by with its furnace already lit but dampened down ready to be stoked up for immediate use. This was quite a contrast to modern day diesel engines which can be started up immediately. The engine-house was about 20 feet long and built of old stonework. It stood on its own track running parallel to the site of what used to be the main track, now the By-Pass. Appropriate points would have been manipulated manually to enable the engine to branch onto or off the main line as required. There were buffers inside the engine house which were to prevent the engine from over-shooting the end of the line inside. If you were to stand on a winter's morning in low sunlight, it is still possible to read on the curved arch of the doorway of this engine house the painted inscription, although now faded, 'GOD SAVE THE KING'.

Females Ploughing

Not far from the engine house, but on the Old Belfast Road to Comber, I recall seeing in the late 1950s a unique sight of two women manually pulling a standard size plough in a small field by the roadside. I got off my bicycle to watch this scene. The girls were strong lasses and they had improvised harnesses around their shoulders. There was a man walking behind the plough guiding it. Because of the distance between the plough and the man controlling it, the girls were not able to operate right down to the roadside but stopped some yards short and restarted the drills at right angles to the previous direction so that the entire plot of ground was neatly ploughed. This manual operation would only have been possible if the ground was soft and the area being ploughed relatively small. I later witnessed this same practice being operated on some small holdings in Donegal. On one occasion a young boy and a girl were harnessed to the plough.

Victorian Post Box

Further along the Belfast Road, Comber just where the Ballyrainey Road branches off, are two small cottages and on the adjacent wall alongside is a post box built into it with the letters VR which dates back to Victorian times when Queen Victoria was on the throne.

Victorian Post Box, Comber, October, 1993.

Non-Subscribing Presbyterian Church

On the right hand side of Mill Street going towards Comber Square are very ornate gates. Stone steps lead from the gates up to this church formerly known as the Unitarian Church. These steps are very well worn and give some indication of the age of the church. The site was formerly known as Windmill Hill as a windmill was positioned there. Mr James Andrews owned the land and the windmill, this land he presented to the congregation as a site for the church. Mr James Andrews was the father of the Rt. Hon. John Andrews J.P., former Prime Minister of Northern Ireland.

The foundation stone was laid in 1838 (although the congregation was formed some years before) and when the Church was due to be opened that year the event had to be postponed because of severe damage due to a terrific storm. This storm was known as 'The Big Wind' which hit Ulster on the night of 6th/7th January when the top of the windmill was blown off and landed on the roof of the newly built church. After repairs, the opening finally took place on the 1st March 1840. The Manse alongside the Church was built in the summer of 1858.

In 1988 the Church celebrated its 150th Anniversary.

Non Subscribing Presbyterian Church Gates, 1993.

Non Subscribing Presbyterian Church, Comber, 1993.

Posting Master — McDonald's Shop

Further along Mill Street, Comber, also on the right hand side going towards Comber Square direction is a grocery shop which always caught my attention. The name above it is J A MACDONALD but alongside it are the words POSTING MASTER. I have often wondered what the history of this was as I do not recall ever having seen these words before over any other building. A suggestion is that it may have been a Posting House where perhaps post was collected from here in the olden days by jaunting car for delivery and in later years by stage coach.

McDonald's shop showing Posting Master sign, 1991.

Comber Cricket green with two black stones in the foreground, September 1993.

The Black Stones

Although Mill Street continues on to The Square, half way along it changes its name to Castle Street and on the left hand side just at the top of Castle Lane there was a cow tail pump which has long gone. Also here were positioned two 'black stones'. These were large stones which were unearthed during the sinking of wells in the area and it was decided it would be easier to let them stay. They were used by the locals for sitting on. In fact it is said that the smoothness and shine of the stone was caused by the rubbing of the men's trousers as they sat on them over the years. In later years when this area was being bulldozed for road widening, the stones were about to be destroyed and some of the locals stepped in to prevent this happening. Instead they were taken down to the Cricket Ground, Castle Lane, where they remain to this day and are still being sat on by spectators at cricket matches.

Comber (North Down) Cricket Club

The ground of this famous and well renowned Cricket Club is also known as 'The Green' which stems back to the time when it was actually a Bleaching Green used by the Andrews Spinning Mill. The Club owes its very creation and existence to the benevolence of the Andrews family who in 1857 provided the ground, formed the Club and ran it. It is now 136 years old and is the second oldest Cricket Club in Ireland. Lisburn Cricket Club which celebrated its 150th anniversary a few years ago is believed to be the oldest. The Andrews family continued to support the club down through the years and Mr Willie Andrews who was a former member of Marylebone Cricket Club brought his expertise and drive to North Down. In fact this gentleman presented a stained glass window to Comber Non-Subscribing Church which was dedicated on 10th March 1919 in memory of his family and depicted a cricket bat and ball.

Fifty years ago the Club bought the ground from the Andrews family and it still retains its prominence in cricketing circles today.

Trading Names in Comber over the last 50 Years

*** STILL TRADING**
**** OVER 50 YEARS AND STILL TRADING**

THE SQUARE

McWHINNEYS BUTCHERS** — SITE EXTENDING TO CASTLE STREET.
JAMES NIBLOCK (CHEMIST) — LATER — HAROLD PORTER (CHEMIST)
(SITE EXTENDING — J. C. GOUCK (CHEMIST)
TO CASTLE STREET) — STRICKLANDS (CHEMIST)*
SAMMY EDWARDS (GREENGROCER) LATER — MARLENE'S FASHIONS
— NOW VACANT (SEPT. 1993)
ULSTER BANK*
DONNELL'S RESTAURANT*
CAMPBELL BATES & CO (SOLICITORS)*
BRIAN McCLEARY (CENTURY 21 — ESTATE AGENT)*
WILLOW TREE COFFEE HOUSE* (ABOVE McCLEARY'S)
M & J HORNER (CHEMIST)*
BOYCES PUB — LATER — GILLESPIE ARMS*
TRENDS UNISEX SALON (HAIR STYLISTS)*
PROGRESSIVE BUILDING SOCIETY*
ERNEST KANE & SON (GARAGE/MOTOR DEALER) — STILL TRADING AS KANE OF COMBER**
THE NORTHERN BANK**
TOM MURPHY (MILKMAN) — NO LONGER TRADING
McMILLEN'S FUNERAL UNDERTAKERS:-
LATER — THE SPAR SHOP (E.&S. McBRIDE)
— McALPINE'S FLOWER SHOP — NOW MOVED TO CASTLE STREET
— ALEX STEWART PARTNERSHIP (SOLICITORS)*
McMILLENS PUB — LATER — ULSTER ARMS (McBRIDES BAR & RESTAURANT)*

CASTLE STREET: (L.H. SIDE FROM SQUARE)

TOM & LILY QUINN (GREENGROCERS — DECEASED)
HAROLD PORTER'S SWEET SHOP — LATER HI SWEETIE
LATER FISH EMPORIUM
(SEPT 1993 VACANT)
CLASSIQUE*
MARTIN SMITH (BARBER — DECEASED)
MARGARET SMYTH (FASHIONS)*
CASTLE FISH & CHIP SHOP — LATER ROULSTON'S BAKERY*
SMYTH & McCLURE (GROCERS — NO LONGER TRADING)
MISKELLY (NEWSAGENT — DIFFERENT SITE SAME STREET)**
EXECUTIVE DRY CLEANING*
J. AINLEY (JEWELLERS)*
THE WOOL SHOP (ED WALKER)*
CASTLE HEALTH STORES*
COMBER SPORTS CENTRE*
COMBER TRAVEL CENTRE (TRAVEL AGENTS)*
SMITHS THE BUTCHERS — LATER — POST OFFICE/SCRIBBLES*

STRAN SECURITY SYSTEMS*
XTRA VISION (VIDEO HIRE)*
IRENE'S (CLOTHES)*
TIM MARTIN & CO (ESTATE AGENTS)*
McCREA'S (DENTIST)*
GRACE BOAL (DRAPER) — LATER LOWE'S FASHIONS**
THE CASTLE INN (LOUNGE BAR — DIFFERENT OWNERS)**
WORLD OF BOOKS*
MOLLY TOMPSON (DRAPER) — DECEASED
THE FLORAL FOUNTAIN (FLORISTS)*
THE BIG BITE (CHIPPIE)*
B. WRIGHT (BARBER)**
WILLIAM BENNETT (JEWELLERS) — LATER — ORRS TRAVEL/ESTATE AGENTS
— MARGARET McALPIN (FLORISTS)*
McGRATHS FRUIT SHOP — LATER — JOHN DOWDS FRUIT SHOP
— H. MAWHINNEY (BUTCHER)*

(R.H. SIDE FROM SQUARE):-
JAMES NIBLOCK (HARDWARE/CAKE SHOP — NO LONGER TRADING)
McMASTERS — COSTUME JEWELLERY (NO LONGER TRADING)
JOHN DONNAN (TAILOR) —DECEASED
DONNANS SWEET SHOP — LATER TSB BANK (RENAMED FIRST TRUST)*
PIPERS FRUIT SHOT* } ON SITE OF OLD
HARRY FRAZERS (FISH & CHIPS)* } COMBER CINEMA
F A WELLWORTHS (SUPERMARKET)* ON SITE OF NEW COMBER CINEMA
HALIFAX PROPERTY SERVICES (ESTATE AGENTS)*
V G STORE — LATER — THE PRICE IS RIGHT (HARDWARE STORE)*
McQUITTY BROS (ESTATE AGENTS)*
HUTTONS (TILE SPECIALISTS)*
ALBERT ANDERSONS (HARDWARE) — LATER — TYNANS FARMER SUPPLIES
— LOWDENS FARMER SUPPLIES*
GARY GIBSON (ESTATE AGENT)*
K J GARDINER (SOLICITOR)*
SEW 'N' SEW*
ALTOS HAIR DESIGN*
WINIFRED GOURLEY (INSURANCE BROKER)*
EXPRESS PIZZA*
DODDS BOOT & SHOE REPAIRS*
MARTIN McCLENAGHAN (BUTCHER)*
GILMORES — FUNERAL DIRECTORS*
MAYFLOWER — CHINESE RESTAURANT*
MEN ONLY — BARBERS*
THE JADE DRAGON — CHINESE RESTAURANT*
JEANIE McROBERTS (DRAPERY & CHINA) — LATER McCREAS FURNITURE
— STRAINS WALLPAPER SHOP*

CASTLE LANE
BUS DEPOT — LATER — DOUBLE GLAZING FIRM
— T GILLESPIE (FURNITURE)*
COMBER AUTO PARTS*
ALBION LTD (STITCHING FACTORY)**

MILL STREET — L.H. SIDE TOWARDS ARCH:-

WILLIAM McGREEGHAN (FRUIT & VEG)
LATER — WINSTON MULHOLLAND (GROCERS)
— SHELIA SCOTT (FASHIONS)*
JEANIE GLOVERS SHOE SHOP — LATER — NANCY McGREEHAN (SHOE SHOP) NO LONGER TRADING
HUTTONS (SWEET SHOP) NO LONGER TRADING
TOM McKEAG (SHOE REPAIRS) — NO LONGER TRADING
THE CD COMPANY (COMPACT DISCS)
W SMITH (PAINTER & DECORATOR) — NO LONGER TRADING
CAROLINE FASHIONS*
JAMES SPIERS (CHEMIST) — LATER JOHNSTON PHOTOGRAPHY (MOVED TO CASTLE STREET)
W J WHITE (ICE CREAM/CONFECTIONERY)
LATER — KNOWLES ICE CREAM PARLOUR
— DAVEYS ICE CREAM/CONFECTIONERY
— ICEBERG ICE CREAM*
POST OFFICE — MOVED TO THE SQUARE — THEN CASTLE STREET
LUCKY HOUSE (CHINESE RESTAURANT)*
THE GAS WORKS — NO LONGER TRADING
PEDAL POWER*
THE LOFT*
W J MACDONALD (GROCER/POSTING MASTER/GENERAL MERCHANT)
LATER — R. MORROW (GROCERS/HARDWARE)
— CONTINENTAL KITCHENS*
— CRAIGS FRUIT & VEG*
AGGIE MARSHALLS FRUIT & VEG (DECEASED)
THE PIN CUSHION*
CRINKLES HAIRDRESSER*
SAM BROWN (BARBER — DECEASED)
THOMPSONS HALL (1904) — LATER COMBER TECHNICAL SCHOOL
BOB GALBRAITH (GROCER) — LATER — MACE SUPERMARKET*
JUST SEW*

R.H. SIDE TOWARDS ARCH:-

TERRY SCOTT (BOOKMAKERS)
SHAWS (DRAPERS) — LATER — JOHNSTONS (DRAPERS)
— MARTIN PHILLIPS (CARPETS)*
CROSBIES TAXIS — LATER — HUGH STEWARTS TAXIS (NO LONGER TRADING)
HARRY McKNIGHT (GARAGE)**
ALSO JOHN KYLE (AUTO ELECTRICIAN)*
COMBER PET STORES (W McBRIDE)*
D H BUSINESS SERVICES*
SALEM GALLERY/TEA ROOMS*
J MIDDLETON (PETROL STATION/BICYCLE/BATTERIES)
LATER — JET PETROL
— BURMAH SELF SERVICE PETROL STATION*
TEMPLE FURNITURE*
FRANK SHAW — COAL MERCHANTS — LATER — TOM CORKEN (MOVED)
— J B COMBER WISE HIRE*

J B PRIESTLEY (GROCER) — LATER — LOUIS ADAIR (GROCER) — MOVED TO DARRAGH ROAD)
W SKELTON (ELECTRICAL GOODS) — DECEASED
ALBERT CLARKE MARINE (BOATING SUPPLIES)*
MORRISONS BUTCHER SHOP — NO LONGER TRADING
ULSTER AERIALS*
CAPTAIN SMITH (CHEMIST) — LATER J C GOUCK (CHEMIST)*
CROSSANS (NEWSAGENT)*
TOM CORKEN (COAL MERCHANT)**
MRS WHITE (SWEET/TUCK SHOP) — NO LONGER TRADING
TOM MACDONALD'S PUBLIC HOUSE — LATER — J BURGESS (PUB) — TOURIST TROPHY (TT) LOUNGE/BAR/RESTAURANT

BRIDGE STREET — R.H. SIDE FROM SQUARE:-
J LIVINGSTONE (NEWSAGENT)*
QUINN'S (GREENGROCER) — NO LONGER TRADING
STRAINS BABY & CHILDRENS WEAR*
UNCLE TOMS CARRYOUT (CHIPPIE)*
EVELINE'S CAKE SHOP*
MARIE'S HAIR STUDIO*
GETAWAY TRAVEL*
MARTINS (DRY CLEANERS)*
STANLEY RACING (BOOKIES)*
JEAN'S FRUIT & VEG*
BARRY MILLAR (MILK DAIRY)**
COMBER VIDEO LIBRARY*
HERRONS — COUNTRY FRIED CHICKEN*
THE BLACK CAT (DRESS SHOP)*
GOLDEN FLOWER (CHINESE RESTAURANT)*
S K ARMSTRONG (OPTOMETRIST)*
BARBOUR & PAYNE (FINANCIAL ADVISERS)*
SPACE DYERS — LATER — N.I. CARPETS*

L.H. SIDE FROM SQUARE:-
NEEDHAMS — ELECTRICAL SHOP — LATER — HORNERS (CHEMIST)*
ANDERSONS (GREENGROCER) — LATER TOM CONWAY (FOOD) — NO LONGER TRADING
MOLLY'S (LADIES FASHIONS)*
SCRABO ELECTRICAL — LATER HCR ELECTRICS*
McWHINNEYS (BUTCHER)*
MUNNS (GROCER) — LATER — PREMIER WINES*
'FIRST & LAST' PUB**
McILVEENS (SHOE REPAIRS) — NO LONGER TRADING
MUNNS (GROCERS) — LATER — PREMIER WINES
MUNNS — PUB — LATER — 'FIRST & LAST' PUB
STRICKLANDS GARAGE

LOWER CRESCENT (FROM SCHOOL):-
CINDY'S SALON*
CRESCENT STORES (GROCERIES)*

SARAH MILLS (BREAD SHOP/LIGHT GROCERIES) — NO LONGER TRADING
FRED WARNER (BLACKSMITH) — NO LONGER TRADING

HIGH STREET: L.H. SIDE FROM SQUARE:-
TOPPING LEISURE (SPORTS EQUIPMENT)*
MULBERRY INTERIORS*

R.H. SIDE FROM SQUARE:-
TWYMAN (VET — NO LONGER TRADING)
CORNFIELDS ART SHOP*
KOSI-DOWN — CONTINENTAL QUILTS/SOFT FURNISHINGS*
H EARNEYS (GROCERS — NO LONGER TRADING)
WILLIAM BENNETT (FURNITURE/FURNISHINGS/HARDWARE)
LATER — R N LUDLOW — KITCHENS/BATHROOMS*
W J WHYTE & SON — HOUSE FURNISHERS*
AGGIE THOMPSON (SWEET SHOP — DECEASED)

MILLVIEW
ANNIE CAMPBELL — GROCERIES/CONFECTIONERY/SMALL CAKES (DECEASED)
ANDREWS SPINNING MILL**

BELFAST ROAD
JAMES MIDDLETON & SON (GARAGE/MOTOR DEALER)**

KILLINCHY STREET — L.H. SIDE FROM SQUARE:-
COMBER INTERIORS (ANTIQUES/ORNAMENTAL GARDEN EQUIPMENT)*
RIVERVIEW SERVICE STATION*

KILLINCHY STREET — R.H. SIDE FROM SQUARE:-
COMBER COMMERCIAL CENTRE (TRUCK & VAN RENTALS)*
THE COOPERAGE (CRAFTS/GIFTS/ANTIQUES)*
EDGARS (CONFECTIONERY) — NO LONGER TRADING
THE GREEN HOUSE (BEDDING PLANTS/TREES/SHRUBS)*
THE MEWS GALLERY*
COSTERS (CONFECTIONERY/LIGHT GROCERIES) — NO LONGER TRADING

PARK WAY:-
COMBER GLASS & PICTURE FRAMING*
COMBER BUILDING CENTRE & JOINERY WORKS*

John Andrews Spinning Mill, Comber

I feel I cannot write about Comber without mentioning the long standing firm of John Andrews & Company Limited. I think the town and its people owe a lot to the Andrews family over the years for providing employment on a large scale to so many from 1863 to the present day.

The finished product from this Mill is linen yarn. The flax is now imported from Belgium but formerly it was home grown. This involved a long process. The flax was pulled and the stalks gathered in beets (bundles) and stooked to dry out. Drying out took place for about two weeks. The next stage was retting when it was put into the dams or oblong 'lint-holes.' Stones were laid on top to keep the flax submerged in the water. Retting took up to two weeks and produced a pungent smell as the flax started to rot on the outside. When this process was completed, the unwanted woody part of

Andrews Spinning Mill as seen from the main road leading up to High Street, 1991.

Main Mill showing Ground, First, Second, Third and Top Floors, 1991.

Entrance to Comber Mill, 1991.

the flax having rotted away, it was then dried out and transported to the scutch mill to be hammered and hackled, turning it into tow. Back at the Andrews Mill it was then put through the further stages ending up as the final product of reels of yarn.

Hot and cold dams as well as the nearby river supplied the mill with industrial water for the spinning process of the flax. In earlier years this water was also fed to the boilers where it was turned into steam to heat the mill. A large well in Railway Street supplied the drinking water to the mill.

Like all other industries in the past, working conditions in the Mill were antiquated and up to the early part of this century 'half-timers' were still being used. 'Half-timers' were children from the age of 12 who were taught in the Mill Schoolhouse, on the ground floor of the premises, for the first half of the week. They then worked in the Mill for the second half of the week which included Saturday mornings. Once they reached 14 years of age they worked in the Mill full time. In 1920 the Government made it illegal for children to work until they reached the age of 14 and this ended the employment of 'half-timers'.

However children were still taught in the Mill School and the

Tow loft where tow is stocked, 1991.

Cold dam, now disused, 1991.

various Church schools until 1938 when the new Comber Primary School was opened. The school in the Mill consisted of two classrooms. Below the gatehouse was a door in the wall which led into a hall. The wide wooden stairs on the left led up to the classroom on the first floor. This was a large room which was divided into sections for different class grades. At the back of this room was a door which led into the other schoolroom which housed the infants and 'bumps'. The 'bumps' was the name given to the toddlers which would be the equivalent of the modern day playschool. The last Headmaster in this school was Mr. Murray, and his daughter Carrie and Miss Crowe were two of the teachers. Miss Murray and Miss Crowe transferred to the new Primary School when it opened.

The Mill was first powered by a huge steam engine. An example of this same engine can still be seen at The Ulster Museum, Stranmillis Road, Belfast. The discarded boilers which drove the steam engine can still be seen on the Mill premises. These boilers were powered by furnaces.

Coal was brought to the furnaces by rail on a private branch line

Disused boilers, 1991.

Thomas Andrews who went down with the 'Titanic,' 1912.

which went directly to the Boiler House. Part of this line is still visible to this day.

The factory horn which summoned the start and ending of the working day was sadly scrapped around 1987. The horn was blown in 1912 to alert the district on the night of the 'TITANIC' disaster. This was a very sad time for the Andrews family and for the people of Comber as Thomas Andrews who was then Managing Director of Harland & Wolff — the builders of this most famous ship of all time, was one of the notable people who went down in it that night. The Andrews Memorial Hall was built as a Memorial to Thomas Andrews and was paid for by the people of Comber. This building is now used as a primary school.

With the kind permission of the present Thomas Andrews, son of the late Mr J L O Andrews, I was taken round the Mill by Mr Bertie Frazer in October 1991 and allowed to take photographs. Bertie has worked in the Mill Office all of his working life to present date and is a mine of information of its functions past and present.

Bertie Frazer in mill office, 1993.

Disused railway track with crane in background, 1991.

We started off at ground level outside. Here Bertie pointed out to me the early, now discarded, coal burner steam powered units. Three of these were always working and two on standby reserve. The original large steam engine was scrapped when electric motors took over. There is still evidence of the railway siding lines earlier mentioned along which coal was transported by rail into the boiler area. There is also here a unique little crane which is still in very good order.

At one part we could overlook the dams which were once used in the processing of the raw flax.

Part of the complex which Bertie pointed out at the frontage of the premises with its own gateway on the same side as the main entrance, once housed the stables. In earlier times the horses would have been used for transportation purposes.

Through the gate at the Main Entrance on an outside wall is a War Memorial recording the names of those mill workers who lost their lives, along with the names of those who also served and survived.

On the ground floor is a workshop containing wood lathes used

Mill showing former stables complex, 1991.

Wood turner Jack Mawhinney working at bobbins, 1991.

for the making and repairing of wooden bobbins of six to eight inches diameter.

As we proceeded from the ground floor we climbed up the stone steps. This was in an older part of the building and I was struck by how much these steps dipped in the middle, worn by countless feet, through the passage of time. The banisters at various steep turns were very strongly built of iron. On the First Floor we entered the Machine Room. My first impression was of rows and rows of what looked to me like sporrans (the workers were quite amused at this description). They were in fact sections of processed yarn. There was a lot of noise from the machinery and the workers were all wearing ear muffs.

On the Second Floor was No. 4 Spinning Room. This is also known as the LINMACK room because of the more modern LINMACK machines. The girls were working at long winding machines. Each girl was in charge of a number of these. The floor was wet and vapour was spraying out from overhead drum devices. The moist air gives the processed yarn more strength as it is wound onto the bobbins. It also gave a fog-like atmosphere in the room. Remains of the original mechanical pulley drive system — no longer

'Sporran'-like processed flax in machine room, 1991.

Machine room — processing raw flax, 1991.

Girl working in LINMACK Spinning Room, 1991.

LINMACK Spinning Room, 1991.

Winding department, 1991.

Dorothy Hanna operating savio winder, 1991.

Girl at winding machine — final stage, 1991.

Carding room — one of the processes in tow yarns, 1991.

Carding room — combing tow, 1991.

Girls at work in No. 4 Spinning Room, 1991.

Machines in Spinning Room, 1991.

Roving Frame in Preparing Room No. 5.

Preparing Room, 1991.

Girls at work in No. 1 Preparing Room, 1991.

Isobel Burgess at work with oilcan, 1991.

View of main yard from No. 4 Spinning Room, 1991.

used — are still in position hanging from the ceiling. There was a strange but not unpleasant smell from the material in this and upper rooms.

The Third Floor was similar to the Second Floor but had more modern types of winding machines. The floor here was also damp but the machinery was not as noisy.

On the Second and Third floors vertical tubes with curved tops constantly travelled along the length of the machines reversing automatically at each end. These tubes were sucking any dust or other foreign bodies from the atmosphere.

The Fourth or Top Floor had winding machines in full production. These were electronically operated and as the temperature of the reels was very important the girls were continually lubricating the machinery with a special oil can. There were also large square overhead mirrors mounted at a slight angle to enable the machine operators to observe the yarn being wound on the opposite side of the machines as well and to watch for any breaks occurring on either side of the very long machines. If a break occurred in the thread, the operator would rejoin it by a knot, laying level each end of the break thus hardly any excess lump was noticeable on the reel. The heat in this room was greatly reduced.

At one end of the room was an inspection area and here a circular amount of material could be hung over a polished three inch rod and the quality of the material was thoroughly examined by Manager Bob Orr.

In all the rooms bright strip lighting gave abundant illumination devoid of any flickering. I was impressed with the large safety doors, well marked, which gave access to lower floors in the event of a fire. The safety doors opened outwards and I actually went outside one of these and stood at the top of the steel stairway which gave me a wonderful panoramic view.

We then went on to the roof. From here I had a closer look at the tall chimney. Bertie told me it had been even taller, having been reduced by 10 to 14 feet of its original height.

At the entrance to the Works at roof level is a very ornate wind and compass weather vane which I would loved to have seen through binoculars for more detail.

We made our way down to ground floor level again and Bertie took me into the office. There I was shown samples of some of the

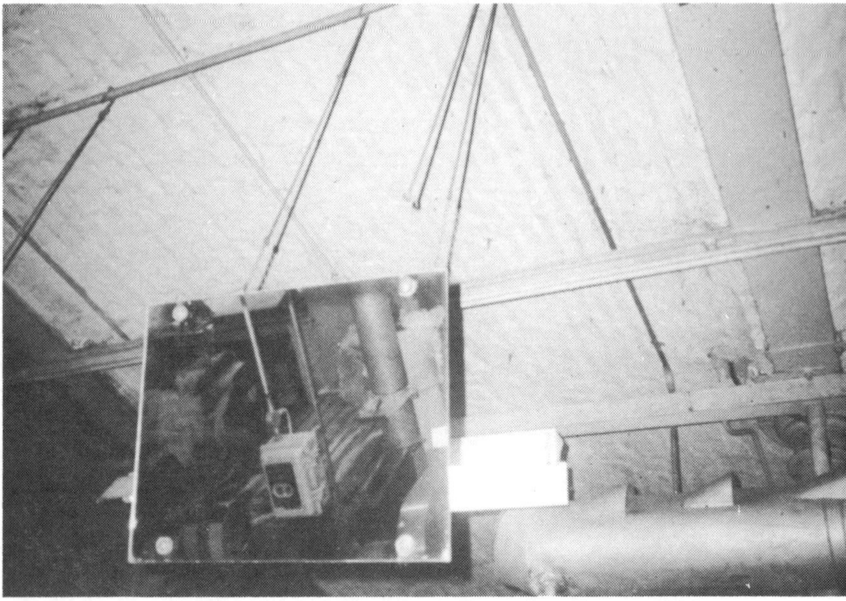

Overhead mirror in No. 1 Preparing Room, 1991

Top floor Winding Room, 1991.

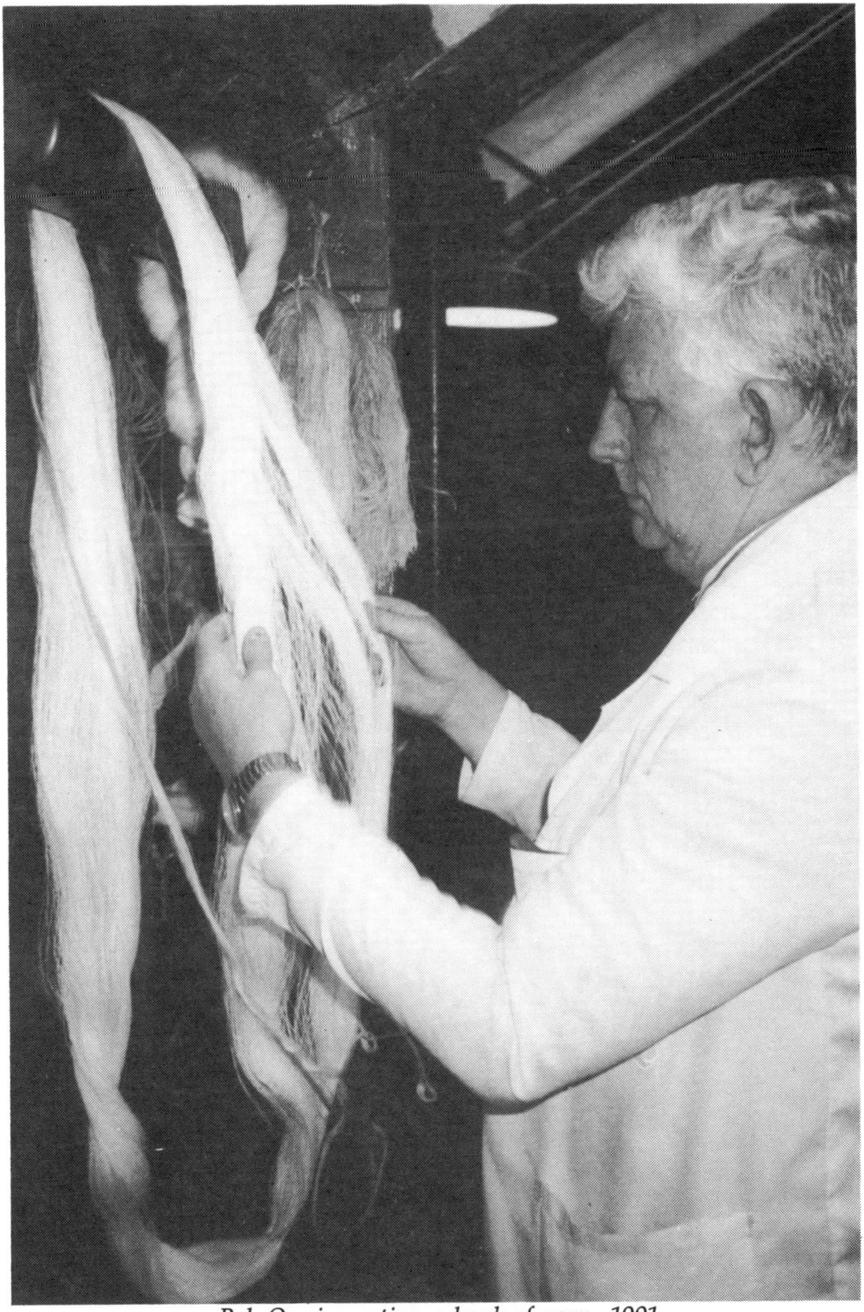

Bob Orr inspecting a hank of yarn, 1991.

Comber Mill showing factory chimney, 1991.

Gauges from disused steam boilers, 1991.

Finished yarns in mill office, 1991.

Cartons of yarn ready for distribution to customers, 1991.

finished reels of yarn in different colours, thicknesses and strengths as they would leave the factory. Framed on the wall were previously used temperature gauges.

The Ards (Tourist Trophy) Race

This was an event known more popularly as the 'TT' which helped to put Comber on the map. The first race was held in 1928. It started about the Quarry Corner in Dundonald along Bradshaw's Brae into Newtownards to Conway Square, along South Street to Comber Square and then unto the Belfast Road towards Ballystockart and on to Dundonald Village and back to the start at Quarry Corner. The circuit covered a distance of 13 miles and was almost in the form of a triangle DUNDONALD - NEWTOWNARDS - COMBER - DUNDONALD.

The race was held annually for 9 years from 1928 to 1936 inclusive. The reason for its cessation in 1936 was sadly due to a bad accident on the approach to Newtownards when one of the cars went out of control and as a result eight spectators were killed and fifteen injured.

This race was famous internationally and sported such famous drivers as EARL HOWE, MALCOLM CAMPBELL, KAYE DON, local driver JACKIE CHAMBERS and many others along with well known, now nostalgic car names such as 'FRAZER NASH', 'RILEY', 'MERCEDES BENZ,' 'LAGONDA', 'MASERATI', 'ASTON MARTIN', 'ALFA ROMEO', 'M G MIDGET', 'BENTLEY' and others.

The Belfast Road where our house is situated was actually part of the circuit. In fact when we were in Tenerife on our honeymoon in 1968 one of the other guests at the hotel, Jim, when talking to us was delighted to hear that Rita came from Comber as he had been the mechanic for Prince Bira and had participated with him in an Aston Martin at the T.T.

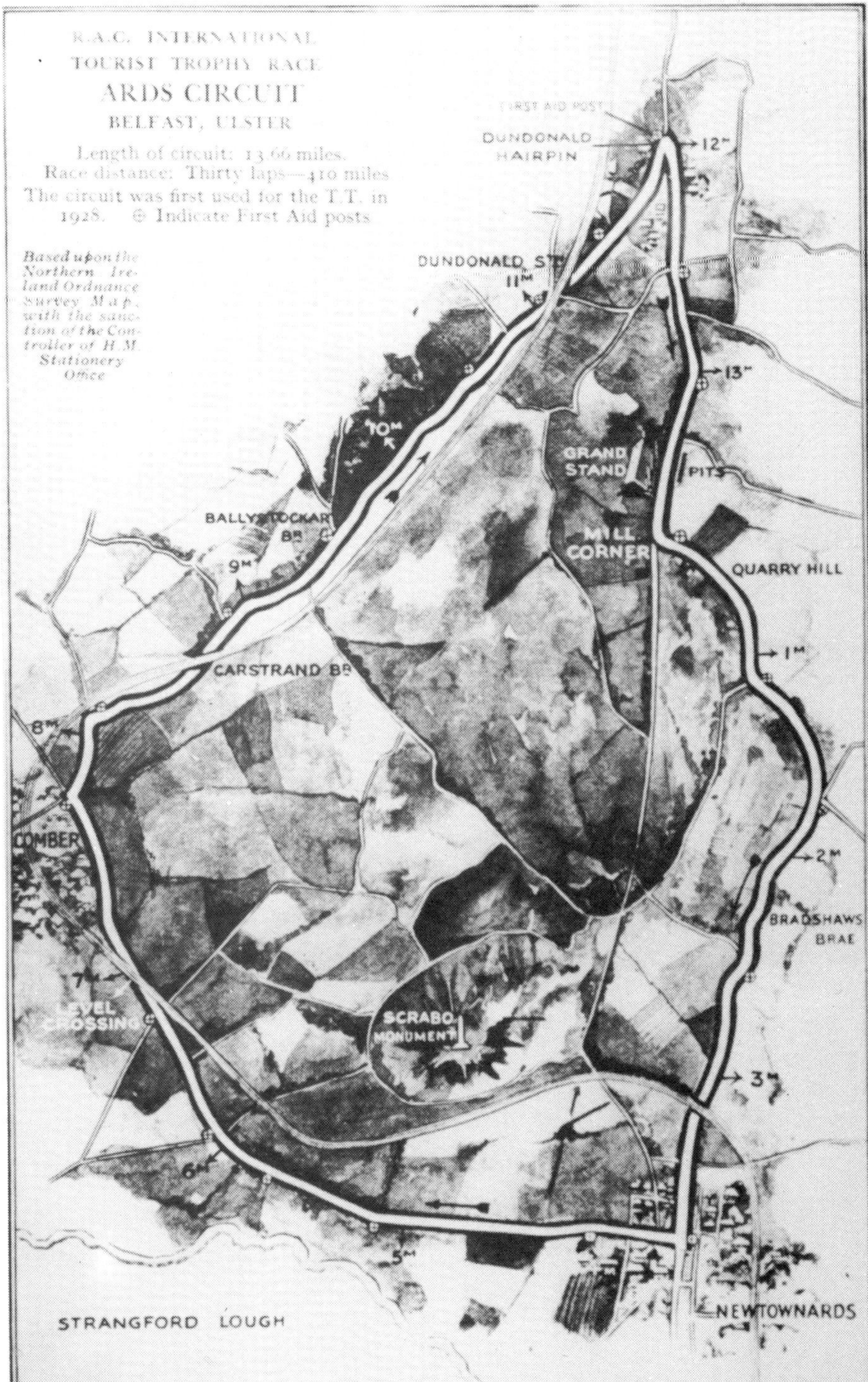

Circuit map of Ards T.T.

Start Area of Ards T.T. at Quarry Corner, Dundonald, 1928. Thistlewaite in a Mercedes Benz is ahead of Baron L. D'Erlanger in a Lagonda.

Drivers and mechanics getting ready for start of Ards T.T. Race, 1929. In foreground Eddie Hall's Arrol Aster (No. 61), Norman Garrad's Aster (No. 60), Stanley Weight's Ford (No. 59) and George Masterson's Ford (No. 58).

RAC Scoreboard, Ards T.T. Race, Dundonald, 1929.

R. S. Outlaw in a Riley manoeuvring corner, Comber Road, Dundonald, 1929.

Count Connelli in a Bugatti(No. 56) heading for corner at Central Bar (now Elk Inn), Dundonald opposite cowtail pump.

A. Divo in a Bugatti entering Conway Square, Newtownards, 1929.

C. R. Whitcroft in a Riley at Francis Street, Newtownards, 1931.

R. Carracoila in a Mercedes Benz along Newtownards Road, heading towards Comber Square, 1930. Notice train on left.

R. Carracoila in a Mercedes Benz behind R. S. Outlaw in a Riley passing Comber Square, 1929.

Brian Lewis in a Talbot behind Campari in an Alfa Romeo. Niblock's chemist shop on right. McWhinnery's butcher shop on left, 1931.

Mongin, Clarke and Field in Delahayes head up Main Street, Comber towards the Belfast Road, 1936.

Rita and Noel on the left along with Jim (the mechanic for Prince Bira) and his wife Anne, Tenerife, 1968.

Prince Bira of Brunei.

The Methodist Church

This church is situated in Bridge Street, Comber. In 1820 the congregation of Methodists had become so large it required the erection of a Chapel. The site was secured from the Marquis of Londonderry and work commenced. It started off being named as Methodist Mission Chapel as indicated on the plaque built into the stonework on the outside of the church. Round the outer ring of this plaque are the words 'GLORY TO GOD IN THE HIGHEST AND ON EARTH PEACE GOOD WILL TOWARD MEN.' Below this is engraved 1820. This would date the church at 173 years old.

R Lee Cole records in his book (period 1860-1960):-

"Comber Mission Station was one of 38 who received an annual grant from the Irish Conference. Before this it was governed by the English Conference and was regarded as part of the overseas work of the English Wesleyan Missionary Committee."

C H Cruickshank records in his book:-

"COMBER — The Church was formerly opened on 22nd December 1822 when Messrs Charles Mayne and John F Matthews preached to crowded congregations."

Methodist Church, Comber, September 1993.

In 1871 the church changed its title from Mission Station when the Irish Conference took over.

Over the porch doorway of Comber Methodist Church another date of 1891 is engraved into the stonework which would perhaps indicate this extension being built.

The Christian Advocate dated 18 August 1905 records as follows:-

> "Rev Charles H. M. Clayton gave his farewell address on 11 Aug. 1905 on the occasion of his leaving Comber."

The Christian Advocate dated Sunday 30 July 1920 records as follows:-

> "COMBER — Church was built in 1820 by Rev. Matt. Lanktree, had been newly painted both inside and out, celebrated its centenary."

The Irish Advocate dated 23 April 1926 records as follows:-

> "COMBER — New Vestry opened on Thursday evening. Contingents from Knock, Holywood, Bangor and Newtownards attended. The Rev. E. W. Young led in Prayer."

The following little poem recalls a lot of the history of Comber such as the trains, the oak tree, Comber Point to Point Races, the cinema, and the dances in Andrews Memorial Hall.

'OLD COMBER'

(TO TUNE: GALWAY BAY)

SOME DAY I WILL GO BACK AGAIN TO COMBER
THE FIRST TIME THAT I GET THE WEATHER FAIR
TO SEE AGAIN THE CARS GET JAMMED IN BRIDGE STREET
AND TO SEE GILLESPIE STANDING IN THE SQUARE

WE'LL NEVER SEE AGAIN THE TRAIN GO BY THE CROSSING
OR SEE THE IRISH OAK IN CASTLE STREET
THAT'S SOMETHING THAT THE OLDER ONES REMEMBER
WHEN THEY'RE RESTING ON THE COUNCIL'S SUMMER SEAT.

WE USED TO GO EACH YEAR TO SEE THE COMBER RACES
TO WATCH THE HORSES RACING ROUND THE TRACK
WE ALWAYS HAD A PICNIC BY THE RIVER ENLER
I WONDER WILL THEY BRING THE RACES BACK.

THE PLACE FOR US TO GO IN COMBER WAS THE PICTURES
AND THINKING OF THAT ALWAYS MAKES ME SORE
FOR WHERE WE USED TO LOVE TO GO TO SEE THE MOVIES
IS NOW A GREAT BIG MAMMOTH SUPERSTORE.

EACH SATURDAY NIGHT THE DANCE WAS IN THE BIG HALL
WE HAD TO GO EACH WEEK THAT WAS THE RULE
BUT WHEN WE TOOK A NOTION TO GO THERE
WE FOUND IT WAS THE COMBER INFANTS SCHOOL.

SO NOW WE HAVE TO SAY GOODBYE TO COMBER
THE TRAIN HAS GONE SOME THIRTY YEARS AGO
THE COUNCIL SKIPS ARE STANDING IN THE STATION
IT'S A COMBER THAT THE OLD FOLKS HARDLY KNOW.

HUGH MAWHINNEY
BUTCHER,
MILL STREET, COMBER.

Alex Murdoch on 'Perfect Chance' at Comber Races, 1930s.

Comber Point-to-Point Races

The races referred to in the poem were the Point-to-Point which were held every year at Mount Alexander, Comber, in the 1930s. They were widely supported from far and near by all horse racing enthusiasts and spectators.

Alec Murdoch, winner, on 'Perfect Chance' at Comber Races being led by Mr. King — father of Osborne King, 1930s.

A lot of the older residents of Comber will know or remember the following little rhyme:-

MONEYREA FOR BAPS AND TEA
BALLYGOWAN FOR BRANDY
MAGHERASCOUSE FOR BREEDING SOWS
AND COMBER IS A DANDY

AUTHOR: UNKNOWN.

Scrabo Tower

The name 'SCRABO' comes from an Irish word meaning a rough or scraggy hill. The basalt ground and hillside surrounding the tower was formed by volcanic activity and evidence of lava deposits can still be seen to this day.

The tower which is a familiar landmark in County Down is 41 metres high and its walls a metre in thickness. It was built in 1857 from Scrabo Hill stone and sandstone. It was paid for by contributions from the local inhabitants as a tribute to the Third Marquis of Londonderry who was held by them in very high regard especially at the time of the potato famine in Ireland. It can be seen for miles around. I myself have seen it from the top of Slieve Donard but it has even been seen from as far away as parts of Scotland. It must be by far the most painted landscape in County Down. Before the days of the Chocolate Easter Egg it was always a most popular site for children at Easter time to trundle their dyed or painted eggs down the hillside. Whin blossoms were widely used for dyeing the eggshells in those days. The act of egg rolling at Easter time was a religious biblical symbol of rolling away the stone from the sepulchre where the body of Christ lay after the crucifixion. Sadly this custom seems to have died out with the arrival of the chocolate eggs.

One morning in 1956 my friend Eddie Hunter and I cycled up to Scrabo Tower. As it was not due to open until later in the afternoon, we parked our bikes at one side of the main door and spoke to one of the two sisters who lived in the tower. Apparently there were three sisters called Elizabeth, Jean and Agnes Millen and two brothers, but I only ever remember seeing two of the sisters. They lived in a neat dwelling inside the tower over to the right hand side of the door. On the left was the stairway up to the top of the tower.

We decided to take a walk until opening time and went across the rough ground below the Golf Clubhouse and there I showed Eddie the large bell that was fitted at a blind spot near one of the greens. This large bell was of heavy cast metal and was rung to warn other golfers of golf balls being projected over the blind hill. Unfortunately this bell was stolen in later years.

We made our way back to the tower and met one of the sisters again and were given permission to ascend the stairway. My first impression was of the acute climb, turning always to the right in a spiral direction. Some distance up the stairway we met the other sister. She was scrubbing the internal steps of the stairway and was making her way down having started up at the strong door at the top of the tower. She requested us to ensure that we closed the door again at the top as quite often she had to go up and close it when visitors left it open. We first went down and carried fresh water up for her before going to the top ourselves. Some of the internal floors were missing and the doors on the stairway of these were securely boarded up. We went through the door which gave access to the walkway on the bastion outside which surrounded the tapered apex. The apex was fitted with red lights which to this day are lit all through the hours of darkness as a warning to approaching aircraft.

It was very cool at the top and a steady breeze was blowing from the South. The view was much more impressive than that of Helen's

Scrabo Tower, 1961.

Lady scrubbing the steps of Scrabo Tower, taken from top of Tower looking down, 1953.

Tower, in that it was much higher and nearer Strangford Lough, thus giving a more spectacular panoramic view. This was because Scrabo Hill in itself was on very high ground and then the Tower rose above that again. On looking downward one had a feeling of the immense drop down to ground level of the tower and even further down to the area of Newtownards and surrounding districts.

We could see quite clearly the aerodrome at Newtownards and were able to watch several gliders being towed up into the air by a power winch situated at the aerodrome. One of the gliders actually managed to gain enough height to soar around the top of the Tower. Using the thermal of rising warm air to maintain sufficient altitude it continued circling for almost an hour before descending gently and landing on the grass area of the aerodrome again.

Eddie and I gazed downwards where we could see the other sister scrubbing the outside steps at the entrance of the tower while their two dogs lay nearby. We could also see our bicycles which looked quite small from our high vantage point. This unusual scene was too good to miss so I held my camera over the parapet and took a photograph of the lady scrubbing the steps with one of the dogs nearby. We also noticed when looking down to the entrance steps of the tower, the existence of what seemed like sunken steps or walls which may have been of an earlier period.

We carefully closed the door on our way down from the bastion and again met the other sister near the bottom steps. We bid time of day with her. The sisters provided tea and cakes for visitors for a small fee but on this occasion we were there too early to be served. I wondered at this stage how many visitors would ever imagine the effort required to scrub each step and the lifting of heavy buckets of water to the top to work down.

We descended the very steep road on our bikes from the Tower to the crossroads below and studied the very interesting little brass cannon that was situated at the crossroads. It was unusual in that the bore of the gun barrel was of quite large diameter of about six inches while the length of the barrel was only about twelve inches long. Alas this cannon has also disappeared. About 200 yards from the crossroads stood Killynether Castle surrounded by trees. It is now demolished but at that time it was used as a Hostel for cyclists, hikers etc. This hostel was renowned for being haunted. Jackie, a friend of mine, had stayed overnight with one of his mates. However, because the hostel had been full up on this occasion, Jackie and his friend were allocated a room at the top of the building. They were quizzed by the warden next morning if they had experienced an unknown presence of a woman. The warden was so hard to convince that they had neither seen or experienced anything unusual that Jackie showed signs of his annoyance.

Chapter 2
NEWTOWNARDS

Ards Hospital

As a result of the 1838 Poor Law Act, 130 Workhouses were built in Ireland within ten years of the passing of this Act. Newtownards was one of these and a three-building unit was completed in December 1841.

Medical Practice began in the Infirmary building of the Newtownards Workhouse in 1842.

Three years later with the tragedy of the potato blight and the scourge of the subsequent famine, more and more paupers were declared and required the shelter of the Workhouse. During the second half of the eighteen forties it became necessary to extend each of the three main buildings. Two large wings were added to the front building and additional infirmary wards were built. As the famine continued to take its toll, further extensions were added to the Infirmary building.

In 1845 the Fever Hospital was opened. Until the turn of the century all patients treated in the Infirmary and Fever Hospital were Workhouse residents. This changed after the Local Government Act of 1898 became law and direct admissions to the Infirmary were permitted. Horse-drawn ambulances were used in the 1900s.

The dual-purpose Workhouse Infirmary continued until 1922 when the Workhouse residents were transferred to Downpatrick. *They actually walked the 29 miles as no transport was provided for them!*

In 1932 the Newtownards Workhouse became the ARDS DISTRICT HOSPITAL.

An extension of one room in the main block provided an Operating Theatre. Buildings and huts were erected during the years 1940-45 for the treatment of wartime casualties. These were later adapted for nurses accommodation and maternity patients. The gas cleaning station incorporated into the out-patient department later became the day room for P.N.U. (Psychiatric Nursing Unit).

In 1940 the McKelvey Pavilion for children which was a gift from

Ards Hospital, October 1993.

Miss McKelvey was opened.

Grant House (named after the Rt. Hon. Wm. Grant, M.P. who was Minister of Health at the time) was opened in 1951 for Midwifery and Gynaecology but was immediately taken over for surgery. The Fever Hospital was closed and improvements were made to the laundry, boiler house, nurses home and mortuary.

With the advent of the Health Service in 1948 the name was changed to ARDS HOSPITAL and Bangor and Crawfordsburn Hospitals were associated to make the North Down Group. In 1954 the Fever Hospital was re-opened as Adair House (named after a former chairman of the Hospital Committee) for midwifery.

In 1957 the McWhinney Hall was opened — mainly from a legacy received several years previously and the Nurse Training School building was opened. Also dual purpose buildings which had been erected previously for the reception of nuclear bomb casualties were adapted for laboratory, radiology and physiotherapy. The Thomas Bailie Ward (named after a former Chairman of the Management Committee) was adapted for trauma, ophthalmology and dermatology. This is now Male Medical Ward.

In 1958 Boyd House (named after Mrs Boyd — a member of the

Committee) was opened. This was an adaptation of the war-time nissen huts and is still in use as an excellent geriatric unit.

In 1960 the Psychoneurosis Unit (P.N.U.) was adapted from the former Out-Patients and X-Ray Departments. Also the Rural Council vacated their offices and these became offices for the Hospital Administrator and the Board Room.

In 1967 conversion of new day room in medical wards became Coronary Care Unit.

In 1968 the Accident and Emergency Unit opened and in 1972 the Calder Theatre (named after Mr A M Calder, M.B., F.R.C.S.,

The brick chimney adjacent to the Ards Hospital complex, 1993.

the first Surgeon and Medical Officer in Charge) was opened. This was partly paid for by voluntary subscription.

In 1974 The Scrabo House Geriatric Unit was opened and an extension to this for the Day Hospital was built in 1988. In 1981 the Medical Records building was added to the Out-Patient Unit.

In 1989 Grant House was reconstructed and an extension of the former Nurse Training School was built to make the Day Hospital for P.N.U. Also Medical Wards and Coronary Care Unit were upgraded.

Now the Ulster, Ards and Bangor Hospitals are linked in one group — the Ulster, North Down and Ards Hospitals Unit of Management.

Adjacent to the grounds of Ards Hospital stands the ruins of an old mill with an unusually shaped brick chimney. It is unique in that it is square shaped. Most chimneys I have seen are either round, or six or eight sided. The chimney is now disused and actually has a dangerous bend in it due to old age. It has metal strips round it for support. Mill Street, Newtownards takes its name from this mill.

The Old Cross, Newtownards

The Old Cross, Market Cross or Newtownards Town Cross in High Street is a unique structure which always fascinated me with its unusual shape and size. I have never been able to find out its original purpose but one of the locals did tell me that Charles II was proclaimed King at Newtownards in the mid 1600s even before he actually inherited the throne. On the occasion of this proclamation claret actually flowed from the spouts of The Old Cross. That must have been quite a day in the history of Newtownards.

Silver City — Ards Airport

In the mid 1950s Silver City Airways was a small company operating between Newtownards and England using Bristol Freighters. These planes had large twin radial engines with a high wing, single tail and conventional style fixed undercarriage i.e. two wheels at front and one tail wheel.

The large rounded nose of the plane opened up to each side

The Old Cross, Newtownards, 1993.

allowing two motor cars to be driven up the ramp and into the fuselage. The doors were closed and securely locked while the car drivers and passengers entered through a bulkhead into a very small cabin with seats. The pilot was situated above the car deck at the front and could talk to the Control Tower by radio.

On one occasion when I was watching, I witnessed the aircraft being delayed by the second car not arriving on time. The plane actually took off with only one car on board. It did its customary circle above the aerodrome. This was a safety precaution then in vogue by all planes against possible engine failure, a practice no longer necessary due to the reliability of modern technology. As the plane was circling the aerodrome the second car arrived. The plane was recalled by radio to land again and the ramps were fitted by an irate member of staff when the take-off procedure was repeated once more. This time the plane continued on its journey.

Silver City "Bristol Freighter," Ards Airport, 1955.

Concrete Pill Box

On the same day as I watched the Silver City aeroplane taking off I also cycled down to the end of the aerodrome over to the ex-army concrete pill box complete with its heavy steel door. The slits around the pill box gave an excellent panoramic view out over the lough. This pill box was one of many built around the lough shore as a look-out for enemy aircraft during the last war when it would have housed a heavy machine gun.

Gliders

Also in the 1950s a small flight of engineless gliders made use of the aerodrome facilities mostly on Sundays. These were usually operated by members of the Air Training Corps. The gliders which had no wheels were connected by a long cable to a mechanical petrol driven winch. As the winch cable was rolled in on a drum this gave lift to the glider which rose high in the air when the pilot disconnected the cable which fell to the ground. The glider then continued on its engineless flight. On one occasion I was at the pill box mentioned earlier when one of the gliders took off and caught an ascending thermal of warm air which enabled it to circle Scrabo Tower for over an hour before descending to the aerodrome. As I watched the whole procedure I wondered if the pilot was trying to break an endurance record. As the glider grounded the metal skid (in place of wheels) took the impact as it slid along the ground and when it came to a stop it lay over gently with one wing touching the ground. The pilot then climbed out after a successful flight.

On another occasion I watched an incoming glider which because of the prevailing wind had to approach the pill box from the direction of the lough. He misjudged his landing height and ended up having to land on the lough shore. Luckily on this occasion the tide was out. I along with others immediately ran towards him but we were all relieved to find he was not hurt and the glider was not damaged.

Chapter 3
HOLYWOOD

On the Belfast side of Holywood a short distance from Palace Army Barracks on ground where the large Sullivan Upper School complex now stands, was a German prisoner-of-war camp during the Second World War. It was possible to see the prisoners still wearing their German uniforms walking around the confines of the tall barbed wire enclosure, while up in raised sentry boxes overlooking the enclosure were British Army guards equipped with guns and searchlights.

Later when the war was over and the deserted prison camp along with other old buildings were demolished, I read in the Belfast Telegraph that while this area was being cleared a bulldözer had broken into an underground tunnel which was being examined. The next day I cycled down to the site as by this time I was becoming very interested in caving. The experience of exploring in Holywood quite appealed to me. Some of the local children took me to the hole where the excavator had broken through. So armed with two torches I climbed down into a dry brick lined passage. The roof was curved and the bricks were of red baked clay. As I walked along the passage I could hear the children calling to me and I in turn answered back. I came to a junction and found an iron framed doorway but without the door. This had been removed from its hinges and was lying inside the cell. The internal measurements were roughly akin to a household garage and contained an iron bed, iron seat and over in a corner was a modern lavatory. Other cells there were of similar construction, one of which was badly damaged. All were in almost total darkness except for a high corner ventilator through which fresh air was penetrating. In the cells I could not find any form of electric lighting, so with a final glance around I headed back along the passageway and was helped out by a large crowd of children who informed me of several men going down the previous day.

Steam train passing through Kinnegar, Holywood, 1950.

I wondered who and why people were imprisoned in such conditions as it was a considerable distance from the prisoner-of-war camp previously mentioned. I do not think they were in any way connected with each other.

Although the grounds were levelled it is quite possible that the prison may still exist underneath in the same condition as I saw it some forty years ago.

On one occasion in 1950 I happened to be in the area of Kinnegar and was lucky to have my camera with me to photograph a steam train en route to Bangor.

The Maypole

I was fortunate one day in the early 1950s to be cycling through Holywood on my way to Bangor when I came upon a traffic diversion in Holywood itself. Part of the main street was closed and a large crowd had formed at the High Street and Shore Street junction. The occasion was the erecting of a replacement Maypole which was laid out along the road on trestles.

The Maypole was 84 feet long and was presented to the town by Mr. & Mrs. W M Dunn and family. The use of a powerful motorised crane was commissioned to lift the giant pole to an upright position and then a squad of workmen very gently guided the pole end into a deep tube already concreted into the roadway. As the pole was hoisted high above the road junction all the onlookers were guided back to a safe distance by the local police. Once the pole was firmly secured, a great cheer went up from the crowd who then surged forward as the official ceremony took place. As the pole was already complete with weather vane, it was necessary to ensure that the cardinal points of the compass were in correct position and this meant turning the huge pole around in its deep hole until the 'NORTH' was correct and given the 'all clear' by a council official holding a small compass in his hand. At this point the crowd gave another great cheer. Within a very short time the main road was again opened to traffic and Holywood returned to normal once more.

I witnessed an earlier Maypole which was donated by the people of Norway which arrived at Belfast Docks by ship and was lowered into the sea and towed down to Holywood by two motor-boats — one at the front and one at the back — to keep it in line while on tow. On a high tide the pole was brought ashore at Kinnegar Esplanade and was lifted out by a petrol driven mobile crane. It was then brought under the railway bridge to its destination.

This was prior to the days of television and when anything like this happened local people and those from further afield would have walked or cycled a long distance to witness such events for themselves.

Holywood Cinema

Only a short distance from the Maypole in Shore Street was a small cinema which was quite unique in that it had the Projection Room built outside the main building over the footpath. The projectionist was able to gain access by means of an external stairway. Occasionally when cycling through the rain on wet nights I would get off my bicycle and take shelter underneath the projection room and listen to the sound track of the film being shown at that time. It could be heard quite plainly from outside the cinema.

The Angry Badger

On again a few miles to where the Culloden Hotel now stands. One very dark night around 1948 my cousin Ernie had missed the last bus home from Belfast to Bangor and had to walk home. Of course there was not the same amount of road traffic in those days. As Ernie approached the Culloden site with high trees on both sides of the road, he was suddenly confronted with a large and very angry badger which growled and grunted and rose up on its hind legs defying him to advance further along the road. Ernie suspected the badger was protecting its young nearby so he tried a dodge of walking quickly to the left followed by his challenger, then reverting back to the right. This he repeated several times and each time the badger blocked his path. Finally instead of changing from left to right he continued to the left but the badger had wrongly anticipated him turning to the right again. This allowed Ernie to take to his heels and get past. When he was well clear he stopped running and continued walking home.

Between the area where the Folk Museum now stands and Rockport near the Girl Guide premises called 'LORNE' there was a high rock on the roadside and here it was possible to drink ice cold water seeping out of the solid rock. This water came from a spring out of the stone and was always a popular spot for cyclists and pedestrians to stop and have a drink. In later years the road was widened in this area so the spring is probably no longer in existence.

Primitive Diving Helmet

On another occasion in 1946 I had an early morning cycle run from Belfast to Cultra on the edge of Belfast Lough. The purpose of this visit was for my first attempt to explore underwater in the open

Primitive diving helmet made out of oil drum and part of WW2 baby's gas mask, 1946.

sea. This was my first and primitive form of underwater diving. For this I used a 5 gallon oil drum on which I had fitted a wartime Baby's Gasmask window. Around the edge of the drum was fastened a long length of lead water piping which gave added weight to the drum to prevent it floating to the surface.

There was a full tide which was to my advantage allowing me to go into deep water very quickly. Clad only in bathing trunks with the drum over my head down to my chest thus providing a crude form of diving helmet I walked slowly into deeper water. As my head started to immerse in the water I was capable of breathing air already contained in the drum on the way down. This lasted for three to four minutes necessitating me to resurface several times to replenish the air in the drum. I did this by tilting my body over to allow the fresh air to circulate which meant I did not have to take the drum off. Crude as it was, it actually worked and for the first time I gazed at the sandy bottom with little creatures gliding around. I was fascinated when a little shrimp swam past me. It was almost transparent. I was overcome with excitement and this was to be the start of a fascinating hobby of sub-aqua diving. I soon had to abandon this first attempt at underwater diving due to the severe coldness of the water as it was in the month of February. I specially chose this time of the year when there were few people about.

When I came ashore I quickly dried and clothed myself. I then had tea out of a flask to warm me up. Some passers-by gave me strange looks but I was so elated with the experiment I did not care and was already planning a proper mechanical breathing apparatus. I soon graduated to a pressurised aqua-lung and the drum was never used again though it is still in my possession forty years later.

John Houston and the Great Dane

On another cycle run to Cultra one evening in the early 1950s I met my friend John Houston sitting in his usual spot in front of Cultra Yacht Club on the seaward side of the road. He was in his Villiers two-stroke engine powered three wheeled open invalid carriage. John had suffered from polio at an early age and was in a wheelchair from the time I first got acquainted with him. He lived at Strandtown in Belfast but drove down every day to his favourite spot. He could not stand up without the aid of crutches. On this particular occasion I found John to be in a very perturbed and frightened state. After calming him down I found on questioning him that a huge dog had jumped upon him and frightened him. When he described the dog I realised John need not have been frightened at all. The dog was a Great Dane which I had met a few times before and known him to be a big 'softie'. I explained to John the dog only wanted to make friends with him. Almost a week later my journey took me past Cultra so I branched down to the sea front and sure enough there was John as usual but lying on the running board of his three wheeled vehicle with its head on John's lap was the Great Dane. John was really contented with his new found friend. In fact for about two years John and the Great Dane were a popular sight to be seen daily down at the seafront. The Great Dane was always willing to help John to eat his sandwiches!

When certain meal functions were held in the Cultra Yacht Clubhouse the Club Steward never failed to bring some goodies to John outside. I always thought this was a very nice gesture.

John Houston at Cultra in his Villiers 2-stroke engine invalid chair, 1951.

John had callipers on his legs right up to his hips and was not able to bend his legs. This was embarrassing to him when he went to the cinema at Mountpottinger called 'THE PICTUREDROME'. The usherettes were always very kind and considerate to him taking his wheelchair and placing it in a safe spot inside for him but he was embarrassed when people tried to get past him when he was seated as he could not draw his legs in. With my engineering experience I decided to try and remedy his predicament. First of all I cut the callipers in two sections, then brazed on bearing joints making locking devices to fit in the area of the knee caps. This gave a hinge-like mechanism allowing John to stretch out his legs or pull them in when required. John was delighted with the result and used this modified apparatus for years.

Handicapped people were at a great disadvantage in those early years as there were few facilities for them either work wise or socially and John had to eventually go to England to get a job. Fortunately as time went on things got easier as the State became aware of the needs of handicapped people and researched into more sophisticated artificial limbs.

The Pile Lighthouse

I cycled down to Holywood from Barnetts Road one summer evening in 1950. My intention was to swim out to the Pile Lighthouse known as the Pile Light which was situated to one side of the shipping lane approximately 4 miles out from the shore at Cultra.

The Pile Light was so named because it was constructed on a concrete base on the sea bed with strong vertical steel stanchions leading up to a hexagon shaped platform. The lighthouse was built on this platform about 12 feet above water level. It was manned by two keepers and their living quarters were to one side below the lantern. A steel ladder led up from sea level to the keepers' quarters. Above these quarters was a large bell which could be manually operated in dense fog. On the top of the lighthouse was a very ornate weather vane. A lifeboat was also positioned on the platform for emergency purposes.

My father swam out to the Pile Light on many occasions with the Swimming Club and this gave me the idea to see it for myself. He told me that at one time it had been badly damaged when a steamship collided with it in a heavy fog. I parked and concealed my bicycle behind a wall and changed into my rubber diving suit but on this occasion I did not use the aqualung.

It was a good two hour swim to the Pile Light where I climbed

Pile Light - was situated between Belfast and Cultra shipping lane

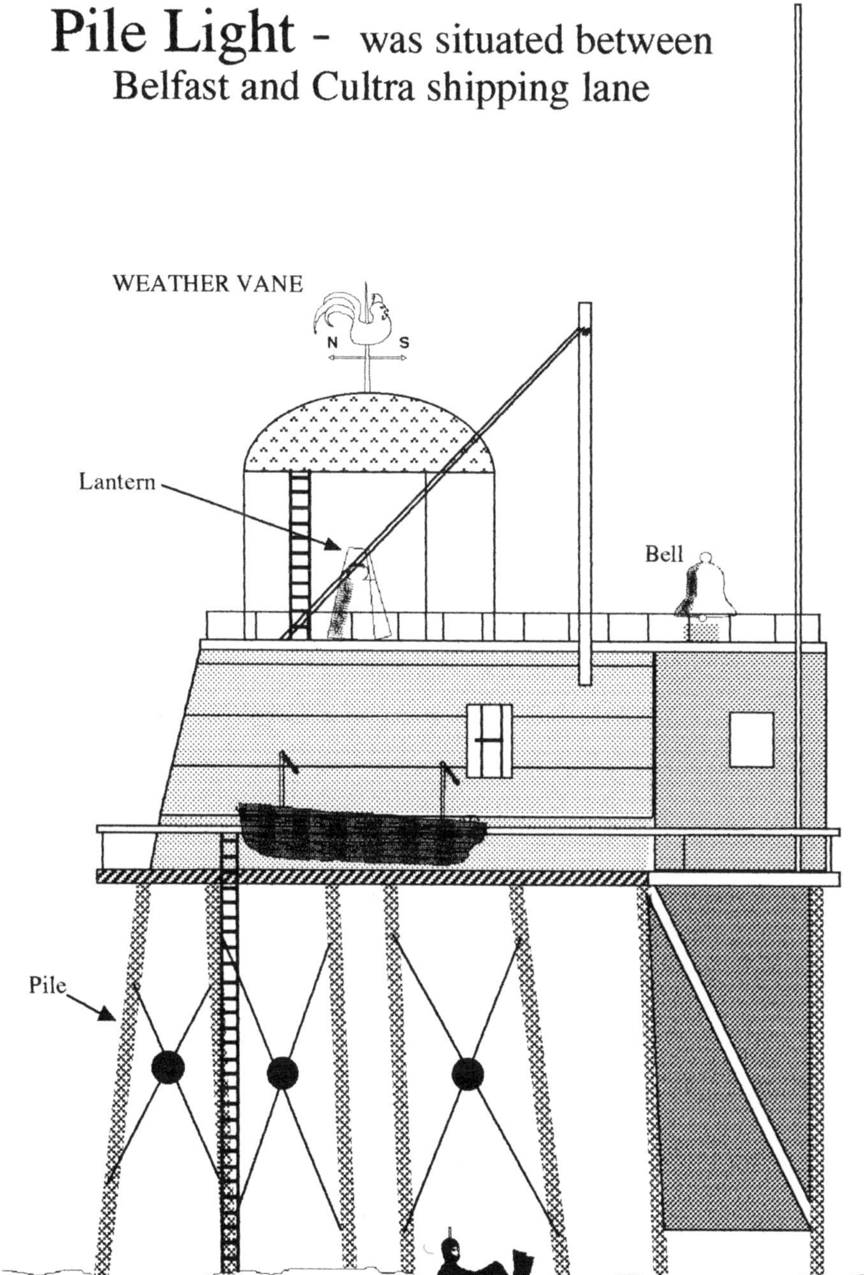

Sketch of the Pile Light.

up the ladder and talked to the keepers who were interested in my rubber suit. After having a chat with them I took my leave and entered the water again swimming back to Holywood. After changing and having a hot drink from my flask I cycled home.

I swam out to the Pile Light on quite a few occasions after that. On my last visit I noticed it had become quite dilapidated with the light flashing continuously even though it was still daylight. Also the living quarters appeared to be deserted. In fact not long after this visit the structure was completely removed and replaced by a more modern string of large unmanned buoys. I was glad I had swum out to the Pile Light before it had disappeared.

Some years later while visiting the Ulster Folk Museum I recognised the weather vane of the Pile Light on display.

The Baby Rook

On one occasion I approached Rockport on my bicycle just where there was a plantation of very tall trees and where each year scores of rooks made nests in the trees to rear their young. I spotted a young rook on the roadside so got off my bicycle to investigate. It was past the fledgeling stage but was confused, so I lifted it and tried to calm it down. I realised it had flown down and could not ascend high enough to the nest. After resting in my hands the young bird seemed to regain its energy so I mounted my bike and holding the bird in front of me I cycled down the hill. As the road started rising again I released the now flapping bird and with its new assisted speed it rose quickly upward and to my joy it landed on the high branches to be greeted by its feathered friends. I knew that in a few days the young bird would gain strength to look after itself.

The Devil's Elbow

At the next bend of the road towards Bangor is the notorious Devil's Elbow and although this has been improved greatly in recent years with widening and banking, it is still a road to be reckoned with. However, just before the Second World War, work was carried out at this very acute bend. A new wide section of road by-passed the bend leaving the old part in its abandoned state but closed off by a pair of wrought iron gates. However during the Second World War a German pilot must have spotted the new curved roadway because high explosive enemy bombs were released and these blocked the new section of road with a huge bomb crater. I and quite a few others climbed down into the crater a few days afterwards just for curiosity. However the Germans were outwitted on this occasion as it only necessitated the council workmen to unlock the existing gates of the 'old' Devil's Elbow bend and traffic flowed without restriction while the bomb damaged road was gradually filled in and re-surfaced.

Chapter 4
BANGOR, CO. DOWN

Giant Sun Fish

In Bangor around the 1930s it was reported that a local steam coal boat had hit an underwater object just after leaving Bangor Harbour. The ship stopped the engine while the crew could be seen hanging over the stern and attaching ropes to a large object. The ship very slowly returned to its berth towing the object behind while the ship's boiler was blowing off steam causing a tremendous roar. As she had been on her way to England the boiler was at full pressure for the voyage but because she turned back she had to get rid of the surplus steam pressure as soon as possible by opening the safety valve. For about ten minutes after she berthed the noise was deafening which brought crowds to the jetty. As the tide receded and the ship was left high and dry, the object which had been towed behind was gradually uncovered and onlookers gasped in astonishment at the giant sunfish which was almost seven feet in diameter and two feet in depth. A large gash in the creature's side which killed it was caused by the vessel's propeller blades. Word quickly went round Bangor where we then lived and my father brought me as a six year old to see this very rare spectacle. The reason for the ship turning back was because of the impact to the propellor blades. I was interested in a very loud tapping noise and my father took me over to witness the surveyor tapping each blade in turn for any damage sustained.

My father expressed sadness at the fate of the sunfish which he said few people would ever see in their lifetime.

Meanwhile the engineers had declared it was safe for the ship to proceed on the next high tide.

The carcass of the sunfish was tied to the ship and on the next tide both coal boat and sunfish left the harbour. At a good distance from land the remains of the sunfish were allowed to sink to the sea bottom where they would not be a hazard to shipping.

Some years prior to this incident before I was born, my father was competing in a swimming race in Bangor from Pickie Pool to the North Pier or New Pier, as it was sometimes called, and back. My father Andrew was then an amateur swimming and water polo champion and a member of the East End Swimming Club and Queen's Island Swimming Club in Belfast. He was also a member of the Ulster Water Polo Team and gave exhibitions of swimming at the Pickie Pool Swimming Galas on Saturday nights. On this occasion because of his rating he was heavily handicapped which meant he was the last competitor to leave Pickie Pool. He swam to the North Pier and touched it (a rule of the competition) and was on his return journey when a large fish surfaced under him. Although at first startled, he soon realised the creature was in fact a porpoise and its only intention was to assist him in much the same manner as dolphins have been known to save drowning swimmers.

Victoria Swimming Club — Noel's father seated (left).

My father did not resist as the lovely creature raised his body higher in the water even though it was difficult for him to perform his leg strokes properly. He allowed the porpoise to guide him towards shallow water where it eventually left him and continued on its way. Incidentally my father did not win that particular race but always talked of this experience with pride!

'Pickie' Pool is said to have got its name from small fish in the surrounding area.

Also about this time my father was preparing along with other swimming club members to harden themselves up for a long distance swim from Bangor across the lough to Blackhead in Co Antrim. Because of the changing temperatures and moods of the lough caused by incoming tides from the North Channel, it was necessary to have accompanying boats for safety reasons during the practices and for the final race along with experienced fishermen with local knowledge who knew the currents and moods of the lough.

The swimming club involved was Queen's Island Amateur Swimming and Life Saving Society of which my father was Hon. Secretary. One important feature of this long swim which was roughly ten miles allowing for tidal deviations, was the procedure to walk ashore at Blackhead and be checked by officials before swimming out to the escort boats for a rub down, warm clothes and hot food. The actual race itself was more a test of stamina and endurance than actual speed and my father was among the successful competitors to complete it.

Egg on Tow

Also about this time my father happened to be walking from home one morning to catch the early morning train from Bangor to Belfast and was approaching a local grocer's shop when he suddenly froze in his tracks. Through a hole at the bottom of the shop door a rat was slowly pulling another rat which was on its back holding an egg in its claws. The rat that was doing the pulling had the other rat's tail in its mouth. My father marvelled at this spectacle. Once they had manoeuvred their way through the hole in the door their speed increased and they continued in this fashion across the deserted roadway. My father's eyes still following them watched as the 'towing' rat avoided the kerb on the other side by using a sloped driveway entrance, then along the footpath some yards before vanishing into the grassy entrance to a field. My father resumed his interrupted walk for the train having then a very high regard for the intelligence of the rodents.

Yacht Aground

Late one evening in the early 1930s word passed round Bangor that a ship was aground on the stones behind the Big Pier. Large crowds gathered including my father, mother and me as a six year old. Our first sight of the incident which was at the back of the Big Pier (which in those days had a large bandstand) was a very large motor yacht lying on her side with twin masts pointing seaward. We watched as Coastguards worked in storm force winds to reduce the damage being inflicted to the yacht. Long ropes attached to the hull were led up to the bollards on the quay wall and as each huge roller pounded the wreck, a group of men drew the strong ropes even tighter. It was a case of preventing further damage rather than trying to refloat the yacht.

Next day the wind abated but sadly the yacht was a total loss. In the following years all sections of it broke up and disappeared except for the heavy iron keel which was collected for scrap iron along with a very large German Howitzer field gun. This Howitzer was a relic of the First World War and stood on a plinth beside the old roller skating rink at Luke's Point. This gun had always been popular with children as it had hinged steel panels in the long body of the carriage. I have fond memories of playing round this gun as well as the one at Ward Park. The one in Ward Park did not fall victim to the scrap iron collection and in fact is still there to this day near the War Memorial and is a centre of attraction to visitors. It was taken from a German submarine in the 1914-18 war.

S.S. 'FAIR HEAD'

During the German air attacks on Belfast and Bangor in the Second World War 1939-45, a large cargo ship the S.S.'FAIR HEAD' owned by the Head Line Shipping Company of Belfast, was severely damaged in the Port of Belfast and the rear section from the hold down to the rudder was towed by sea into Ballyholme Bay and beached for cutting up for scrap.

My cousin Elvin and I were able to enter it one day when the tide was out. We did this by means of the double bottom and were able to gain access to the cargo hold and then unto the upper deck. Part of the cargo consisted of tins of tightly rolled bacon. Some of these were rusted by the sea water.

The 'OREGON'

Another war casualty at this time was the 'OREGON,' though not by enemy action. Incidentally she was quite an interesting cargo ship as she was one of the very early diesel engined models ever built and was among a convoy of ships anchored in Belfast Lough. This convoy was awaiting its naval escort when a violent storm blew up and swept the 'OREGON' ashore at Wilson's Point, Bangor. Sadly she broke in two. The rear section was left on the rocks at the Point while the forward end was refloated and towed to Ballyholme Bay for breaking up. Within a couple of weeks of this I was in a rowing boat in Ballyholme Bay and went alongside the major part of the wreck. Tying up the rowing boat to the wreck which had been purposely holed to prevent it floating off, I clambered aboard and entered the engine room. I had a good look into one of the main engine cylinders. The cylinder head had been removed probably by interested and curious marine engineers.

The 'SAMANCO'

Another ship which was grounded and severely damaged in the same storm was the 'SAMANCO' of approx. 6,000 tons. She was almost new and was a fast modern cargo ship. This ship was ruptured right along the bottom severely damaging the bottom plates. She was grounded to the left of the 'OREGON' but about two hundred yards out from the rocks and as it was considered worth saving, an all out effort was made to salvage her.

First of all it was difficult to ferry salvage men across to the ship in the storm, so concrete blocks were buried in soil on the high part of the bank near a little pumping plant and strong steel wire cables were led from the anchorage on the bank out over the sea and fitted to the stern of the wreck.

Then a walkway with steel mesh side walls was hung from the original cables. This enabled workmen to walk safely from land across to the wreck even in very rough weather. Tons of concrete were poured into the torn bottom of the ship and it was necessary to cut away the huge rudder which was allowed to lie on the sea bed. When the holes in the ship's bottom were sealed she was pumped dry of sea water and the unique swing bridge was removed and powerful tugs towed the 'SAMANCO' away to be repaired for further service. It may still be possible to locate the concrete anchor blocks embedded in the bank and for sub aqua divers to swim down to the huge steel rudder. I did this myself in 1952 and was truly amazed by the sheer size of it. Some sharp steel ribs were still a danger underwater at the rocky bank. These were from the stern of the 'OREGON.'

The 'EVELYN'

At this time a wreck was raised in Belfast Lough also for scrap iron. This was a coal boat called the 'EVELYN' which had sunk as far back as 1913 as the result of a collision in Belfast Lough where she had lain for 31 years. She was also towed to Ballyholme for breaking up. My cousin Walter and I visited her by rowing boat in Ballyholme Bay. It was a rough day in winter and I was able to jump aboard while Walter rowed away and sheltered behind the wreck. I was fascinated to see this boat after her being submerged for so long. All woodwork had gone leaving only the steel hull which was encrusted with all sorts of marine life. I managed to force open the iron door to the engine room and then almost jumped overboard in fright as a blast of hot air hit me in the face. When I recovered my composure I found the salvage crew had left a brazier burning to give them some heat and had forgotten to put it out. A strange sight on the boat was the shiny black coal with no scum deposits at all, which had been in the hold for many years under the sea.

When I was safely in the rowing boat again it was Walter's turn to go aboard. For devilment I said nothing about the fire but watched from a distance as Walter forced open the door. After experiencing the hot air he shook his fist at me as he realised it was a set up.

While rowing gently just clear of the starboard side of the ship I had a good view of a large concrete patch where the bow of another ship had cut deep into the rear side of the 'EVELYN.'

Rail Crash Bangor to Belfast — 10 January 1945

The 10th of January 1945 was a very foggy morning when this disaster happened. The early morning Bangor train was en route to Belfast with shipyard workers. The fog became so dense and visibility so poor that the train came to a standstill near the Oval football ground in the Sydenham area. It was here that another train ran into the back of it. My father and I had left our home in Stormount Street and were walking to work with thousands of others to the shipyard. As we approached Fraser Street Bridge our first indication that something was seriously amiss was the booming sound of warning detonator signals coming from the direction of the Belfast and County Down Railway (BCDR) between Kinnegar and Sydenham and as far up as Dee Street Bridge. On Fraser Street Bridge we stopped along with hundreds of other workers to try and see through the fog what was happening but this was in vain and as we continued on into the shipyard complex we could hear the warning bells of ambulances and fire engines. As we arrived into our various departments and 'checked in' there was a mood of anxiety throughout the shipyard. It was not until 8.30 a.m. that the first sketchy report started to drift through of the train crash. As the morning progressed it became apparent that many shipyard workers had been killed or seriously injured and a great despondency loomed over the Yard resulting in very little work being done that day. A lot of men had their legs broken by the carriages being crushed in concertina fashion. For quite a while after this disaster people did not want to sit at either end of the train, preferring to stay in the centre.

American Assault Landing Craft

Towards the end of the Second World War all around the south coast of England and other vantage points, a vast collection of ships and material was being assembled and checked.

Morningside, Ballyholme Bay, Bangor, Northern Ireland, was one such assembly point and here the soil and stones of the beach were suddenly bulldozed to give a temporary hard access surface.

The mystery was solved within a few days when several large American Assault Landing Craft approached Morningside on a receding tide. They dropped huge anchors from the stern and while paying out cable they headed straight for the beach at speed and ran aground on the sand.

Meanwhile troops were marshalling long convoys of new American Army ambulances and these were guided in batches down on to the sand and driven backwards up into the gaping doors of the landing craft. It was surprising to see the long line of vehicles disappearing into the ships. The inner ramps of the craft were folded inside and the huge doors closed. When the incoming tide once more surrounded the landing craft we heard the ships' engines start up, then the wire hawser took the strain and gradually the heavily laden ships were afloat. Shortly after the stern anchors were drawn aboard and the landing craft headed out to sea.

It was about two months later that the news of the Normandy landing was released to the public and the mystery was solved. So that quiet little area of Morningside in Ballyholme was directly linked with the invasion of France.

American Warship in Bangor Bay 1949

My cousin Elvin Cairns and I set off one evening in 1949 in a canvas canoe from Groomsport to Bangor Bay to get a closer look at an American warship anchored there some distance offshore. As was the policy in wartime there was no name on the warship, just a number. We were intrigued with the detachable booms on each side which enabled the warship's small ferryboats to moor alongside. The sailors walked along the booms to embark or disembark from the ferryboats. To our disgust we noticed a severe leak in the canoe so after taking the photographs we headed with all speed for Ballymaconnell beach and safety. By then it was quite dark as we pulled in the canoe. After turning it upside down to drain the water out we wheeled it home.

American warship showing booms at each side, Bangor Bay, 1949.

Close-up of bridge of American warship in Bangor Bay, Co. Down, 1949.

Bicycle Polo Match in Bangor

One morning in 1950 I had been invited by a friend of mine to go and see a bicycle polo match in Bangor. My friend George was actually taking part in the match.

We left early from Belfast to cycle down to Bangor. I was on an ordinary conventional bicycle but George was on his specially constructed polo bicycle. This polo bicycle was an illegal form of transport on a public road due to the fact it was not road worthy having very small wheels and a fixed wheel gear. Also the machine had no brakes, mudguards, lights or bell. The front forks were almost vertical which allowed the rider to turn at right angles or reverse while cycling.

By the time we reached Bangor I was exhausted with laughter at the antics of George on his peculiar bicycle.

Needless to say his legs were aching with sheer exhaustion as he was not able to free wheel at all, in fact when going downhill he had to use all his energy to hold the machine back by forcing against the pedals.

The venue for the Polo Match was the area where Clandeboye Park is now. I watched the match and saw the opposing teams using all their skills on their bicycles. At one stage from my vantage point I was able to see the ball hurtle through the air lodging itself between the tubular frame and the saddle of George's bike. Of course the players were not aware of this and tempers became very heated and blows almost struck because they could not find the ball. It was only when I drew their attention by pointing out the position of the ball that the game continued.

George's team lost the match and on the way home I had to assist him by pushing on his shoulder at every little rise on the road. By the time we arrived back to Belfast his legs were actually swollen and in a bad state. In fact he did not recover from this ordeal for about two weeks, nor did he ever use the polo bike on the public roads again!

'BALLYGALLY' Steam Coal Boat Leaving Bangor

One early morning in 1957 I was on the North Pier at Bangor when the steam coal boat 'BALLYGALLY,' after previously having

Coal boat S.S. ''Ballygally'' leaving Bangor, Co. Down, 1957.

"Duchess of Montrose" arriving at Bangor Bay, Co. Down, 1957.

deposited her cargo of coal, was heading out for Wales for another consignment.

'DUCHESS OF MONTROSE'

One day in the 1950s I happened to be at the Big Pier in Bangor when the day-tripper 'DUCHESS OF MONTROSE' arrived in from Scotland. Any passengers who wished were allowed ashore for about an hour before the boat did its return trip to Scotland.

Bomb Crater at Ballymaconnell Beach

At the same time as the S.S. 'FAIR HEAD' was bombed in Belfast Docks, a German plane for some unknown reason dropped a high explosive bomb which exploded about fifty yards out below high tide level, left of Ballymaconnell Beach, Bangor. The resultant deep crater was as wide as a house. The sand was all removed by the blast and this caused a clay lined deep pool to be formed which was a hazard to non swimmers and particularly to children. The hole stayed in this state for quite some time but eventually the council decided to dump hard rubbish in it. This was commenced and tons of bricks and stone were driven to the hole daily for disposal. At one stage during this exercise the council lorry got embedded in the soft sand and when high tide filled the bay the roof of the lorry was just visible above the waterline. The water damaged lorry was eventually dragged ashore at low tide. Hard material was laid on the wet sand to give the replacement vehicle a grip until the bomb crater was finally filled in.

Camera Obscura

When I was in my teens I used to cycle frequently down to my Aunt's house called 'Easton' on the Groomsport Road, Bangor. I enjoyed these visits immensely as my cousins were always messing about with boats. In fact my two youngest cousins Walter and Elvin were more like brothers to me. One of the days when I was there I can remember it was very bright and sunny and I went to visit the 'loo' or the 'bogs' as we called it then. Of course in those days the 'bogs' were mostly positioned outside the house. This particular one was in the yard. On this occasion when I entered and closed the door I was astonished to see displayed on the inner back wall of the 'bogs' a perfect picture in full colour, but upside down, of the scene across the road even to the detail of people passing by. This phenomenon is known as 'camera obscura' and is a pin-hole feat of nature which in this instance was projected by means of bright sunlight through the keyhole at a certain time for a very brief period. Apparently I was the first person to witness this and afterwards when there was bright sunlight there was always a race for the 'bogs' but more for the 'camera obscura' than anything else! I have experienced it more recently in my home through a small aperture in one of the Venetian blinds.

Ballymaconnell Point

There is a pleasant walk around the shoreline to Ballymaconnell Point, first climbing the stile into the National Trust property. The outer edge is hard going due to soft wet ground, but on rising ground can be found the concrete support of a wartime searchlight used to light up suspect enemy shipping. Further round is a little bay with an island of solid rock about two feet above high tide but accessible for about one hour at low tide.

On the inner side of the rocky mound can be found the anchor of a wartime patrol ship which was driven inside the area but was lucky enough to be salvaged without damage only leaving its anchor behind in the process.

The little grass and moss covered Jenny's Island is next and is only really an island at high tide. It is accessible by foot when the tide is out. This island is known to botanists for rare plants although I myself could never find anything strange on it.

The 'ANNAGHER'

In the late 1940s my cousin Elvin and I often watched from Jenny's Island the recovery of scrap metal from the sunken cargo boat the 'ANNAGHER.' In December 1937 this boat of about 586 tons was heading for Wales from Belfast in a severe storm. About half a mile straight out from Jenny's Island she went down with a large cargo of scrap iron and only one of the ten crew members survived. Again with the shortage of scrap iron during the last war, a salvage vessel planted four large buoys around the sunken ship to mark the spot. An electro iron magnet was lowered under the sea and was hoisted up again with lots of the 'ANNAGHER's' iron cargo sticking to it. This in turn was dropped into the recovery vessel. This procedure was repeated many times over several months.

About 1952 I was talking to a friend called Albert who was to bring a small motor-boat from Groomsport to Bangor, so he agreed to take me and my friend John out to the site of the wreck of the 'ANNAGHER.' The weather was choppy as John and I dropped overboard wearing full underwater diving gear and we quickly sank to the bottom in about 35 feet of clear but very cold water. A stiff current caused us to cling to the 'ANNAGHER.' We searched about a half mile square on the bottom but only found scraps of jagged steel and a large deep groove which must have been the resting place of the ship before the salvage ship blew it up along with the cargo, removing the lot with the powerful magnet mentioned previously. Meanwhile on the surface Albert was becoming uneasy as the weather was getting very unsettled and he tried to follow our air bubbles as we moved about down below.

At the same time John and I were having a problem as a number of very large stinging jellyfish had been carried by the current in our direction and we had to take great care not to touch them for fear of stings. When we rose to the surface we could see Albert's boat plunging violently. He was relieved to see us surface safely and manoeuvred the boat to give us shelter from the waves. He helped us both aboard and we lay on the floor of the boat to recover while he headed at top speed for Bangor Harbour where we arrived safely in the increasingly rough seas.

Our dive had been exciting and very interesting although we were too late in time to see the 'ANNAGHER.'

The 'PRINCESS VICTORIA'

The night the 'PRINCESS VICTORIA' went down on the 31st January, 1953 I had been cycling that day down to Portaferry, but because of strong winds and blizzard conditions, I found it almost impossible to cycle back on the return journey and had to walk for long stretches at a time. Little did I know of the terrible drama that was taking place on the far side of the peninsula off the Copeland Islands. I would only have been about 12 miles away on the Strangford Lough side of the peninsula but did not hear of the disaster until I arrived home that evening.

The 'PRINCESS VICTORIA' was a passenger and car ferry of 2,600 tons operating between Larne and Stranraer. She had left Stranraer on the evening sailing but was blown off course and in the fiercest of gales she finally capsized and foundered some miles off the Copeland Islands with a considerable loss of life.

The morning after the tragedy I cycled down to Bangor and walked along the rocky edge of Ballymacormick Point. Just at the little sheltered bay before Jenny's Island on the Bangor side, I saw washed up by the storm the upturned hull of a large ship's lifeboat bearing the name 'PRINCESS VICTORIA'. The hull was in perfect condition except for the edging of the rubbing strip which had been torn by movement of the boat along the stony beach while in the inverted position. A rope had been tied from the upturned lifeboat to an iron gate nearby to prevent it floating away on a high tide.

Shortly after I arrived a squad of men including two Coastguard Officers walked around from the Ballymaconnell direction. The Coastguard Officers were wearing wellington boots and they waded into the shallow water attaching two strong ropes to the far side of the upturned boat and leading the ropes across to the squad on the beach who in turn pulled with all their strength until the heavy boat was finally pulled over to a half upright position. The two Officers climbed inside and thoroughly examined every section of the interior including the watertight compartments at each end. After giving a signal, the lifeboat was lowered back again to its original upside down position and I heard them report 'no survivors or bodies inside'. The group continued on towards Groomsport by walking along the extreme edge of the rocks, at the same time carefully examining all the small inlets.

I cycled along to The Orlock and at the bungalow of my cousin Walter Cairns there, we all listened on my little short wave radio to various ships in the area reporting to the Coastguard Station that they had picked up a number of bodies from the sea. As Walter's bungalow was situated next to the Coastguard Station which was on high ground, we were able to watch from this elevated position the Donaghadee Lifeboat doing a controlled sweep of the area looking for survivors or bodies in the water. All the following week the area from Orlock to Ardglass was thoroughly searched.

It was believed that the cause of the fate of the 'PRINCESS VICTORIA' was due to the strength and fury of the waves breaking down the stern doors leading to the car deck and quickly flooding the ship.

Founder Members of the First Ulster Sub Aqua Club

In 1955 I happened to read in the local paper that there was to be a meeting regarding the forming of a Sub Aqua Club in Belfast. I went along to the meeting which was chaired by Dr Douglas Boyd. I found it so interesting I stayed behind to talk to Dr Boyd and told him of my primitive earlier attempts at diving with a five gallon drum fitted with the window of a baby's wartime gas mask. Instead of laughing at me Dr Boyd was quite impressed and showed much

Noel (extreme right, standing) along with other members of Belfast Branch of British Sub Aqua Club which included Billy Rodgers, Margot Sidney-Smith, Maureen McGladdery and Mike Suchard at Strickland's Glen, Bangor, Boxing Day, 1957.

interest in my venture and at this meeting I became one of the founder members of the first Belfast Branch of the British Sub Aqua Club in Belfast diving with them for a period of 10 years. We trained at the Grove Baths. Dr Boyd had negotiated an arrangement that we would use the pool two evenings a week after the general public had vacated the building.

Of course the heat was switched off once the public left and the water got colder and colder as the night went on. Mike Suchard an Englishman was the Club Diving Instructor and Billy Rodgers was the Swimming Instructor. Their training was very thorough and we had to swim so many lengths of the baths with our weight belts on and without fins on our feet.

Each person's progress was logged in their own official book and countersigned by the Instructors until such times as they were

Billy Rodgers (second from left) and Noel (fifth from left) with other Sub Aqua members at Stricklands Glen, Bangor, Boxing Day, 1959.

considered proficient in free swimming and the use of an aqua lung. Part of the training consisted of members being paired off and sharing an aqua lung underwater with one mouthpiece. At weekends we would dive at different venues along the County Antrim or County Down coast and carry out these drills in deep water. With the exception of a couple of affluent members, most of our gear was home made and quite primitive. In fact my first actual diving suit was made by my mother out of a barrage balloon which had been shot down in the Ormeau Park during the Second World War. I thought myself the 'bees knees' in my silver suit and was nicknamed the 'Silver King' by my diving companions!

It was always a tradition for members of the club to do a 'dive' every Boxing Day. Strickland's Glen, Bangor, was always the venue for this event. It was mostly the practice to have hot tomato soup to warm us up afterwards as it was quite easy to heat up. In fact we did this so often that I took a dislike to tomato soup and it is only recently I have been able to take it again.

Jenny Watt's Cave

I don't know how this cave got its name. There are different stories in this respect. One is of a young girl of that name who took refuge in the cave while being chased by a man as far back as the eighteenth century. Another was of an old woman of that name who lived in the cave and was reputed to have been killed by falling rocks. It was also said that the cave stretched across country and almost to the Belfast Road in Bangor. I was always intrigued by this and around 1959 a friend of mine Billy Rodgers and I travelled to Bangor and entered the cold water early one morning in order to make use of a very high tide. I was wearing a 'dry' rubber diving suit with warm woollen clothing underneath and complete underwater diving gear. Billy was only wearing bathing trunks and full diving gear. How he stood the intense cold beat me but Billy was a very hearty and capable long distance swimmer and the cold did not seem to affect him at all.

Our particular objective on this occasion was to explore the cave. It had a very low entrance and by using breathing apparatus we made use of the incoming tide to dispel the mud and debris which we scooped out of the cave entrance.

Billy and I took it in turn using iron bars to scoop away the grit and mud which once dislodged was carried along by the sea water. At times the sediment was quite blinding and we worked in complete darkness using touch as a guide. It was a credit to the aqua lungs that they worked without hindrance in appalling conditions. A hard squeeze on the ankle of one of us was the signal to retire and have a breather while work was continued by the other. As we were working inside the cave in only three to four feet of water our air supply lasted about fifty minutes giving us ample time to make progress. At last the tide receded and we both lay in the now re-opened cave. However after eight to ten feet along it seemed as if the roof had previously subsided and this obstructed our investigating any further along. Regretfully we had to abandon our attempt to solve the mystery of the cave. At the time Billy and I were of the opinion that a second entrance might be found on the other side of the private wall inland but as we did not wish to trespass we were not able to follow through with this theory. We were disappointed at having to give up and swam instead on the surface around to Pickie Bathing Pool and back again. Perhaps some time in the future the mystery of Jenny Watt's cave will be resolved.

Further along the coastline in Groomsport I tried one very dark calm night an experiment just to satisfy my curiosity by diving to the sea bottom in full underwater gear. I was armed only with an underwater torch. There was a lot of fluorescence in the water and as I glided along just inches above the sandy bottom I disturbed little shrimp like creatures which scurried away from my light as I headed out into deeper water until at 30 feet deep I drifted along. At one point I stopped and listened in amazement to clicks and squeaks emanating from little creatures among the seaweed. Several crabs came towards the light with their nippers open and were swimming along before they descended and disappeared into a jungle of seaweed. I always thought before this that crabs only moved along the sea bed. I only saw one small fish and it did not bother to retreat. I noticed the water temperature dropped suddenly at the bottom and for some unknown reason I felt uneasy and turned for land feeling safer at the sea bottom in more shallow water. I glanced at my wrist compass for direction. The pressure in my ears popped as the depth decreased and the shallows were reached at last. Although nothing happened I could not feel as relaxed as I would have been in daylight.

The 'LETITIA'

In 1935 a remarkable coincidence concerning a large liner called the 'LETITIA' of around 13,000 tons owned by the Donaldson Line comes to mind. This ship was on voyage from Canada and calling at Belfast Lough to disembark passengers. These passengers were put on a tender for transport to the Port of Belfast allowing the ship to continue on her outward journey. This journey however was to be almost disaster for the liner. She ran aground just off the coast at Orlock, Co. Down. Along with crowds of other folk, my parents brought me down to see the remarkable spectacle of a large ship aground only a stone's throw away from the shore. I was eight years old and remember the crew wore white outfits and their white caps had twin ribbons attached at the back similar to the French matelots.

It was fortunate that the weather stayed calm and the ship was towed off the rocks four days later and was able to resume her voyage.

The coincidence mentioned earlier was that a young lad called Bobby Brown was one of the passengers who disembarked at Belfast on this same ship two years later.

Bobby had travelled over to live with his grandparents in Belfast just opposite to where I lived. We became great pals and our friendship has lasted to this day. When Bobby arrived we other kids were all in awe of him as he had all the American gear including baseball cap. He had a fantastic pair of roller skates which I think I had on more times than Bobby himself. In fact one day I actually roller-skated from Stormount Street to Cultra and back and this was when the roads were not as smooth as they are today. Needless to say the next morning my legs were so stiff I could hardly walk!

Chapter 5
THE ORLOCK AND DONAGHADEE

Two tall observation masts about thirty feet high with alternating wooden steps gave one a fine view over the sea. The purpose of these masts was to enable the coastguards to climb up them when low sea mist was present to give them a good view over the fog. One evening in 1949 I cycled to this area and noticed there was a low sea fog, so getting off my bicycle and going over to the masts I was invited by the coastguard, who was already on one of the masts, to climb the other one. I was able to hear the coastguard on the mast relaying information as to shipping in the area to the Coastguard on the ground who in turn relayed this information by means of short wave radio to Orlock Coastguard Station.

There were various ships sounding their horns in the area at the time. Even with modern electronics it was safer to use one's eyes for observation. I heard a splash in the water from a ship passing nearby and realised it was one of the crew members 'swinging the lead'. This was the term used for tossing a lead weight attached to a rope over the side of the ship. When it reached the sea bottom he started pulling it up, at the same time counting each length, approximately a yard long, thus assessing the depth. This practice was being used to prevent the ship running aground as it was taking a recognised short cut through the inside of the Copeland Islands.

Although there were no incidents that evening it made me aware of the invaluable service rendered to shipping by the coastguards.

In 1960 I was invited to try and recover a pair of spectacles dropped by an English visitor while he had been on a private boat trip off the Orlock. The Englishman was staying with a relative who lived at Orlock and it was this relative who approached me with the request. Of course I jumped at the opportunity of getting a boat trip out into the lough for a dive. He explained that the boat had been quite some distance out from land when the spectacles were dropped and pointed to the approximate area. I estimated the depth of water to be from 25 to 40 feet and told him I would have to bide my time for calm weather and a slack tide as I have had previous experience of the strength of the currents in that area.

Some three weeks later all was perfect for the attempt.

The Englishman's relative towed me out in his dinghy which was powered by a small outboard engine. The reason for this tow was to overcome the difficulty of getting in and out of the small boat with all my gear on. I was suitably clad in my 'dry' diving suit covering two thick long sleeved pullovers and a pair of woollen long johns complete with rubber gloves, mask, snorkel tube and aqua lung with full air cylinder and heavy lead weight belt. I also wore rubber fins on my feet, an underwater compass on my left wrist and a strong knife encased in a sheaf which was strapped round my left leg. I wore a deflated life jacket complete with small gas bottle which in an emergency could be released by a lever being pulled. The life jacket also had a rubber tube fitted with one way air valve which allowed inflation to be carried out manually by mouth.

Always after a 'dive' when rough weather was encountered, I was able on the return journey to inflate the jacket and swim back to base at my leisure as the inflated jacket kept my face well clear of the waves. However on this occasion it was not necessary.

The boat owner had motored out away from the seaweed and was idling the engine some distance from the rocks and it was no problem for me to swim slowly along on my back with my mask drawn clear of my face. I held on to the side of the boat, enabling me to stay clear of the propeller and chatted to the boat owner as we went along. When we arrived at the spot the boatman stopped the outboard engine and I sank gently to the sea bottom some twenty feet below. The water was clear and the visibility about 50 yards so taking a compass bearing I then began a methodical search of the area by carefully drawing aside clumps of seaweed so as not to stir up clouds of mud and sand. I was amused when little crabs would stand upright and present their open nippers in defiance at my intrusion. At the end of a pre-determined swim I would swim over some yards and return on a new track so covering a large square

Orlock — facing the archway is man-made mysterious roadway underwater, 1961.

area of sea bottom. Although alert for any sign of the spectacles I could not help listening to the sound of little crustacea as they wended their way among the seaweed. I could hear the distant dull thud of the diesel engine of a large cargo boat outward bound from Belfast. The sea bottom changed in character and became rocky with sparse undergrowth. This required careful screening and I occasionally glanced at my pressure gauge to confirm the amount of air left in my cylinder. I came across some tin cans on the bottom and even these had to be examined but to no avail and then with only five minutes of air left in my bottle I spotted the elusive spectacles lying among a clump of seaweed. I lifted them up and carefully placed them in a net bag which was tied to my waist. I then turned over on my back and went some distance looking upwards at the surface of the water until I finally saw the bottom of the boat which had towed me out. I slowly ascended and broke surface in brilliant sunshine. The boatman was delighted that I had recovered the spectacles and as I held on to the side of the boat he started the engine and we were soon back to the beach. I was invited to his home for a well earned dinner and after washing the spectacles he rang the owner in England and promised to post them over the next day.

Some weeks later my cousin Elvin Cairns and his wife Diana carried my diving gear around the Orlock to a lonely inlet beside a short tunnel in the rock. This inlet was 100 yards long by 20 yards wide. The depth of water varied from zero to 40 ft. On diving under the surface in very cold water I found the floor of the inlet was lined with rows of iron bound wooden slabs. Each slab was approximately four and a half feet by three feet wide. The slabs were interconnected to each other. I followed out from land this man-made floor on the sea bottom until it stopped at a depth of around 40 feet. Each slab was still in good condition and very heavy. I was completely mystified as to their use and the expense they must have cost to manufacture. I knew a coach road is alleged to have been built around this area a very long time ago but the wooden floor did not seem to link in with that theory. As I swam back along the bottom of the inlet the water was so clear that as I looked upwards towards the surface I could see Elvin and Diana staring down at me from above. Gradually I increased my depth to 40 feet and then a big surprise awaited me. A large shoal of little fish each about six inches long passed by and to my amazement each fish had a round black ring the diameter of my little finger almost at its tail. As they turned I could see another marking exactly in the same position on the other side. The weird marking was very noticeable when the shoal hovered before changing direction as they appeared to be going in reverse. I assumed this was nature's method of protecting the little fish against predators. I was quite elated with my interesting 'dive' on the Orlock coast and rejoined my friends shortly afterwards. On the way back to their bungalow we called in at the Coastguard Station and mentioned to two of the Coastguard men on duty the strange roadway under the sea but they were not able to throw any light on it. I hope I will learn the purpose of this some time in the future.

TV Novelty

The late 1940s heralded the coming of television throughout England and Wales. Of course at this time it was in its primitive state with only black and white transmission being received and without the modern technology of zoom lens etc. Also aerials were very large and ungainly. At this time television sets were not freely available in Northern Ireland.

Donaghadee was one of the rare areas for reasonable TV reception due to the fact that there were no hills or mountains to interfere with the TV signals. Two enterprising chip shops near the sea front had television sets installed in their premises. Of course only one channel was available but even this was a great crowd puller bringing a lot of business to the two 'chippies.' The two shops had to have elaborate aerial arrays mounted on their roof tops and the signals received were of course subject to interference due to atmospheric conditions when the screen would become obliterated by the condition commonly known as 'snow.'

The TV sets then were encased in large free standing cabinets which stood about 3 to 4 feet high with 12″ screens. When a very interesting programme was on and the atmospheric conditions suitable, it was almost impossible to find a vacant seat in the cafes. The TV sets were discreetly placed by the management of both establishments so that they could not be viewed through the windows. It was a popular dodge for customers to leave a few chips on their plates so that the assistants would not take them away! Indeed on occasions people were known to put in extra orders so that they could retain their seats. The female assistants had a very busy time squeezing past the crowded tables. It was to be quite a few years later before a transmitter was erected on Divis Mountain in Belfast and satisfactory viewing was received in certain areas in Northern Ireland for the first time.

'CATHERINE RENNEY'

While in the Donaghadee area and along the Millisle Road in the vicinity of 'The Commons' putting green, right at the water's edge, I wonder when people are walking along this stretch of rocky shore, if they give any thought as to the origin of broken pieces of tiles which are continually being washed up here. These tiles were the cargo of a boat called the 'CATHERINE RENNEY' which was outward bound from Chester to Belfast in the early 1900's with her cargo of reddish brown speckled fire clay tiles. She was manned by a crew of three men and a young boy. Sadly on this particular voyage the boat encountered adverse weather conditions and was shipwrecked off 'The Commons' and all four crew members were drowned. The Captain's body was returned to England for burial while the good folk of Donaghadee collected money to bury the other three crew members in Donaghadee Parish churchyard.

A large tombstone in the Churchyard records the tragic event although when I last visited it in 1988 the headstone had fallen over concealing its engravings.

The tiles carried in this boat were similar to those used on yard floors of very old dwelling houses and in fact I remember them in our own particular yard in Belfast. They measured approximately 12 inches long by 7 inches wide with a thickness of 2 inches.

Although this tragedy happened in the early 1900's the sea is still washing up tile fragments to this day.

'RUTH II'

About 100 yards further along from the wreck of the 'CATHERINE RENNEY' towards Ballyvester is another wreck. At low tide by the water's edge the rusted remains of a winch and assorted items which belonged to a large four-masted schooner 'RUTH II' can be seen. This schooner was of Danish origin and was blown ashore here in January 1943 when the cabin boy from it was drowned. I swam out to it the following week in my diving suit. Even in her unfortunate state she was still an impressive sight with her four tall masts. She was also equipped with an auxiliary diesel engine for extra propulsion. She was grounded some distance from the actual beach and had been battered very severely against the rocks. As the boat had not broken up there was no spillage of oil in the water and this allowed me to swim around it at the same time staying well clear of the large masts which were already showing signs of collapsing. At the stern I could see the door of the crew's quarters lying open and was able to view the polished woodwork inside. The water was very cold but I did not attempt to board the stricken vessel. I could not afford a camera in those days so regrettably have no pictorial record of this lovely ship.

Cable Station

Further along the road towards Millisle is the remains of an old cable house and on the beach can be seen the armoured telegraph cables coming out of the sea and entering the cable house. A red diamond shaped warning sign was erected on a tall pole on the land adjacent to the water's edge signalling to shipping the presence of the cables on the sea bottom. The cable house itself was unmanned and covered with barbed wire and periodically was opened only for inspection by communication engineers. There was always a light humming sound coming from it. I only saw it open on one occasion as I was passing by on my push bike and stopped to look in. I saw two engineers at work inside but as they seemed to be quite occupied I did not want to disturb them.

Instead I carried my bicycle and climbed over the rocks about 30 yards to the right hand side and found an old drinking well.

St Patrick's Well

The well had a nameplate 'St Patrick's Well.' It was quite small with a protective iron frame round it and a small access door. The water in the well was covered in green algae and was not fit for drinking. On this occasion when I arrived I met a gentleman sitting beside it with a large jar of water which he had drawn from it. He confided that he lived in England with his wife. She had previously lived within sight of the well but was ill at home, and at her request he had travelled across to Northern Ireland to bring back some of the alleged healing waters from it. After talking some time with the gentleman I left him with his thoughts and climbed around the rocky area to an old swimming hut beside a swimming pool which was in a bad state of disrepair.

The Heyn Memorial — Gustavus Heyn

Some yards away from the swimming pool at Ballywhiskin is the impressive monument to Gustavus Heyn. It is in the form of a large granite pillar and inscribed with his name, the date of his life span 1889-1937 together with his Coat-of-Arms. Richard Gustavus Heyn was buried five miles out at sea and the monument faces seaward.

Heyn Memorial, 1950.

He was a previous owner of the firm G. Heyn & Sons. In fact most people assumed that the G. HEYN was actually George Heyn. This firm was also known as the Head Line Shipping Company and the Ulster Steamship Company. It had a fleet of cargo vessels named after headlands on the Irish Coast. Some of the names of these ships were 'CARRIGAN HEAD', 'ROONAGH HEAD,' 'RAMORE HEAD,' 'RATHLIN HEAD,' FAIR HEAD,' BENGORE HEAD,' INISHOWEN HEAD,' TORR HEAD,' and 'BALLYGALLY HEAD' which traded to North America, Europe and the Baltic. The ships displayed the RED HAND crest on house flag, bow and funnel. The ships' Menu Cards also displayed the RED HAND and the origin of this symbol was as follows:

> LEGEND HAD IT THAT IN ANCIENT TIMES THE KING OF ULSTER AND ARGYLL (DALRIADA) ON HIS DEATH BED, BEING UNABLE TO DECIDE WHICH OF HIS TWO SONS SHOULD BE HIS SUCCESSOR IN ULSTER, ORDERED THEM TO RACE ACROSS THE MOYLE; THE FIRST

TOUCHING THE SHORE WOULD BECOME HEIR TO THE KINGDOM. STORM CONDITIONS PREVENTED AN IMMEDIATE LANDING, SO ONE SON UNSHEATHED HIS SWORD SEVERING HIS HAND AT THE WRIST AND THREW THE BLOODY HAND ASHORE CLAIMING HE WAS THE FIRST TO TOUCH THE SOIL OF ULSTER.

The firm sold off the ships in its fleet in the late 1950s/early 1960s but is still in operation to this day in Victoria Street, Belfast.

From this Heyn monument out towards the sea is a gully in the rocks. I have been here on occasions when the tide was very high and also when the tide was very low. About 30 years ago at a low tide I swam in this particular gully and with walls only four feet apart and about eight feet deep I examined the walls and saw lovely sea anemones or 'Bloodsuckers' as they are sometimes called. These delightful creatures are blood red in colour and are quite harmless to human beings. The gully extended some yards out to sea then went into an acute turn to enter the open air at low tide level.

Although it may not be of interest to others, I was quite fascinated with this gully and some years later I entered it again — this time during a high tide and wearing my diving suit complete with mask and snorkel. I watched the little anemones with their tentacles spread out to catch and feed on minute plankton. It is probably their tentacles and vivid colour that frighten people. I could only think at this time of the different visual contrast the gully portrayed at high and low tides.

Chapter 6

BALLYCOPELAND WINDMILL AND FURTHER ALONG THE OUTER COASTLINE

Ballycopeland Windmill

On now to Millisle and a short journey inland. In the early 1950s I went with friends Charlie and John on our push-bikes towards Millisle. My push-bike was power assisted by a 20 cc 2-stroke petrol Cyclemaster engine while the push-bikes of Charlie and John were power assisted with Phillips 40 cc 2-stroke petrol engines fitted just above the pedals.

As we headed towards Ballycopeland I asked my friends if they would like to see inside the Ballycopeland Windmill which was built in the 18th century. They were quite eager to do so.

As on previous occasions I stopped at a roadside cottage about a mile from the windmill to ask permission from the lady there to visit it. After signing the Record Book I was duly given the large door key (which, incidentally, was about 8 inches in length) to gain access to the Windmill and was told to report if there was any damage inside the windmill. We promised to do any necessary tidying up inside while we were there. Of course that was in the days before the Windmill was taken over by the Preservation Society and when it was in a very dilapidated state both inside and out. It had not been in use since the First World War 1914-1918. As I was a regular visitor to the Windmill, we were told to stay as long as we wished since it was a very wet day. We made our way over to the windmill. We brought the bikes inside and closed the door. We left our bikes at the bottom and ascended the very worn and loose stairway, taking special precautions as we did so. The stairs were interrupted by little square landings at various stages. These landings in particular were very unsafe due to dry rot in the wooden

John Wilson examining grinding machinery — Ballycopeland Windmill, 1956.

structure. Parts of the roof of the windmill were exposed to the elements allowing rain etc. to penetrate the interior and birds were nesting among the wooden gearing in the upper floor.

When we arrived at the top floor, although it was in the worst condition and in a very dirty state with bird droppings, it was quite bright with light penetrating the slits in the roof. So after initial cleaning up of this part, we set up our cooking equipment and soon had a meal in progress.

The huge gear drive that transmitted the power of the four large windmill blades fascinated us although the blades were almost non-existent and in such a bad state. A heavy chain was fitted across

Ballycopeland Windmill, 1953.

Inside Ballycopeland Windmill, 1956.

the drive shaft to prevent any movement of the remaining stalks of the blades and also to prevent any visitors being injured by the open gearing equipment in the floors below. After we had a hot meal we explored all the spaces between the floors taking care not to step on the closed double-hinged trap doors on the floors for fear of falling through them. The purpose of these hinged trap doors was to allow the bags of flour to be lowered down through the floors to the very bottom of the tower for collection outside the mill. On the ground floor was equipment for separating the chaff from the grain.

Before we left the mill we each took a floor and started cleaning up. This took about a couple of hours. We accumulated quite a lot of rubbish which we deposited in a huge pile outside the windmill. After checking all was safe, we then returned to the cottage to hand back the large key and sign again the official book. The photographs will give some idea of the condition of the windmill before it was taken over and renovated by the new Authorities.

I was always appreciative of being entrusted with the key on each occasion, allowing me to explore the windmill each time with different friends at our own leisure.

On returning to our journey around the coast, we passed a strange wooden building between the Ballycopeland Windmill and Millisle. This building was about 15 feet high and the same in diameter. The strange thing about it was the six exact sides, one of which had a well made door with a small window. There were three windows in all. The roof was conical in shape and had a little knob at the point of the apex. The roof was coated with asphalt to make it watertight. It was not inhabited so we opened the door and went inside. It was completely empty consisting of one big six sided room. It had a raised wooden floor to prevent dampness from underneath. For whatever purpose this building was used, it was indeed of very sound structure. I could never resist inspecting it each time I passed and I always referred to it as The house of 'Euclid' because of Euclid's theory of six-sided figures.

Radar Towers — Ballyferris

In the 1940s two huge Radar Early Warning Towers were built in Ballyferris where a large caravan site is now. These Towers were for the purpose of locating enemy aircraft and provided an early warning system. They were approximately 200 feet high and each had a round revolving dish similar in shape to the modern TV satellite dishes. These revolving dishes were controlled from a block house. The block house was typical of army design, rectangular in shape and similar to that of an air-raid shelter but with reinforced concrete roof with narrow slit openings on each of the four sides.

When hostilities ceased after the war the site was abandoned and I can remember on one particular evening in the 1950s cycling from Belfast down to Ballyferris in complete darkness. The two deserted radar masts were a good distance from each other and I made my way down a lane to the one which was furthest away. This one still had the dish intact. I parked and locked my bicycle and started to climb the deserted tower. The first 20 feet of steel ladder had been removed, probably to prevent anyone such as me from climbing it. However I still achieved this by wrapping my arms and legs around the stanchions and heaving upwards until I reached the steel ladders above the 20 feet line, when I climbed even higher. By now the illuminated view over the countryside was quite exciting and looking out to sea I was able to spot lighthouses on the Isle-of-Man and England. The climb was tiring on the wrists but I was in for an unpleasant surprise. It started to rain and the steel hand holds were very cold and slippery to touch so I had to abandon my climb and instead headed down the huge structure until the level where the ladders had been removed. These ladders were not like the conventional sort of ladder. They were of a utility design in steel, being one long stanchion with horizontal hand grips welded to each alternate side. These grips were of bare metal and were used by alternate hands and feet when climbing. I was now quite wet and when I wrapped my arms and legs around the steelwork for descending, I found myself starting to slide downwards out of control to the bottom. I suffered friction burns to my hands and legs. Once more, however, safe on terra firma I gazed up at the huge monster and wished I could have reached the top. Sadly it was not to be as when I passed that way again some time later, demolition work on the Radar Tower had already commenced.

Skullmartin Lightship

On now to Ballywalter. Often when I passed through here on my bicycle I would stop at the harbour and gaze out at the red shape of the 'SKULLMARTIN' lightship. She lay at permanent anchorage in deep water about three miles out from the rocky coast just beyond a line of semi-submerged rocks which were a danger to shipping. I often wished then as I looked out to the lightship that I had a boat or access to one to enable me to see it at closer quarters.

The lightship was a focal point on a barren coast and in the late 1940s when I was quite used to long swims dressed in my rubber suit with plenty of old woollens underneath to keep out the cold, I decided to swim out to the lightship. I had given this project quite a lot of thought and sought advice from the local fishermen in Ballywalter Harbour. These were the men with the knowledge and expertise of the local tides and currents. I found them to be very interested and extremely helpful. Their advice to me was to enter the water at Ballyferris at a given time on an outgoing tide. This would enable me to arrive at the lightship half an hour before the tide would turn again.

So early one Saturday morning in July 1950 I cycled down to Ballyferris with my gear. I parked and locked my bicycle in a secluded spot in the small sand hills at Ballyferris. (Sadly these sand hills have since been removed). So dressed in rubber suit, rubber gloves and with rubber fins on my feet which gave tremendous power to leg swimming strokes, I entered the water. On this occasion I did not use breathing apparatus nor did I wear a face mask. On a long journey a mask can be quite sore on the face when not constantly underwater. Of course as a safety precaution I also wore a vital piece of equipment which was a home made deflated lifejacket equipped with a CO2 gas cylinder which could be inflated in an emergency by squeezing a lever. This lifejacket had been an inflatable air pillow which I had adapted for this use. I had attached a small leather harness which enabled it to be strapped over my shoulders and it buckled round my waist. I also had a few bars of chocolate tucked inside the flexible neckband of my suit.

The water was not so cold on the outgoing tide and I quickly swam into deep water. It was a beautiful calm morning with practically no wind and ideal for this venture. I turned around and began swimming backwards in my usual manner when doing long distances, in the direction of the Lightship which was quite a distance south of me. I found it quite pleasant to maintain a steady rhythm and maintained an outward thrust as the 'SKULLMARTIN' now appeared ever closer. There was a lot of scum on the water which is usual on an outgoing tide.

Every so often I would turn around and check my direction, at the same time always being on my guard for any power boats in the area. At infrequent intervals a sudden splash in the water, sometimes quite close at hand, would startle me and it required some will power not to panic. The splashing was usually a fish breaking surface. Basking sharks are known to frequent this coastline and although harmless, nevertheless being confronted with a large fish of this size can cause a feeling of great apprehension.

By now I had almost reached the lightship and could hear the current sweeping past the mooring chains, so by approaching and using the current to propel me I was able to close my legs around the huge anchor chain and hold myself in a comfortable position to observe the now very large looking lightship. I noticed along the side of it the water running down from the scuppers where the keepers had washed down the decks.

The lightship was identical in size and design to that of the ex-lightship 'PETREL' which is now at Ballydorn and used as a Club House for Down Cruising Club. I was quite impressed with the huge mast of the 'SKULLMARTIN' and also the lantern house in the centre of the ship. Two of the lightship keepers came forward to speak to me. They informed me they had been watching my approach for some time not knowing what it was that was moving in the water. They were very interested in the diving suit stating it was the first time they had seen one close up and were quite amused when I pulled out the bars of chocolate. They were even more surprised to see the chocolate bars were quite dry. I showed and explained to them the various items of my suit and equipment. They were quite amused at the name 'cummerbund' which was the waistband on the suit and which allowed the jacket part and trousers of the suit to overlap and be encased by a broad tight ring which sealed the suit making it watertight. They had never heard of the word cummerbund before. The two keepers invited me aboard but regrettably I had to decline, knowing if I did not stay in the water I would find it much harder to re-enter. I chatted to the keepers while waiting for the tide to change which was roughly about 30 minutes. When it was time to take my leave I relaxed my grip on the large anchor chain and the now incoming tide swept me away clear of the lightship in the direction of Millisle. With the cries of 'safe journey' from the two keepers, I resumed my normal swimming position and settled down once again to a gentle rhythm aided by my fins.

I glanced back several times and was surprised how fast I was travelling with the current. The water of the incoming tide was much cleaner but also a lot colder. I had unwelcome company on this return journey in the form of large red stinging jellyfish and was forced to keep my hands behind my neck to prevent getting stung on my wrists. Again I encountered the odd splash of a fish nearby. By manoeuvring my body at a slight diagonal I eventually swam ashore at Ballyferris from where I had started. Standing on the shingle I gazed back at the now far off 'SKULLMARTIN' lightship and thought of the keepers on board. They would have something unusual to tell their mates. Again I was to regret not having a camera with me to record this unusual visit.

I made my way to where I had left my bicycle which was there safe and sound and, after changing, I triumphantly made my way home. I was down at Ballywalter Harbour two weeks later and saw the fishermen to thank them for their help. They told me they had called at the Lightship in their fishing boat and the keepers had told them of my visit and they even mentioned the cummerbund on my rubber suit and of my stock of chocolate in the neckband. They were quite impressed that I had no bother in the very cold water around that coast. They were obviously delighted that the swim had been such a success. I thanked them for their help and advice which enabled me to achieve this venture.

The 'SKULLMARTIN' lightship like others was taken out of service and actually ended up as a pirate radio ship under the name 'THE CAROLINE' in the 1960s. To my knowledge she was eventually broken up in Scotland.

Ballyhalbert Aerodrome

The next place of interest was Ballyhalbert with its old wartime aerodrome. This aerodrome was in continuous use during the Second World War 1939-45. I visited the area several times in the latter days of the war and watched very old worn British Beaufighters and Beauforts taking off on sorties over the Irish Sea. The aircraft were in poor condition and, when landing, sounded like a lot of tin cans, yet they gave reliable patrol service out to sea every day.

For the purpose of the aerodrome the sea front at Ballyhalbert had a row of navigation beacons fitted on steel tubular poles which were embedded in concrete in the water. The poles stood about 15 feet above the waterline and were a guide to help pilots line up their planes to land on the relatively short runway. The runway had two rows of lights at ground level and these, as well as the beacons, were controlled by staff in the glass roofed control tower which was about 20 feet high. The electric cables which were the source of power to the beacons and runway lights were encased in steel tubes for protection. These cables ran from the beacons in the water along the sand to the control tower.

During the landing of the planes, all runway lights and beacons were switched on, even in broad daylight, and switched off immediately after landing had taken place. Once I was lucky to see a red rocket being fired into the sky as a warning and saw the incoming planes turn back out to sea while some object was removed from the runway. The flight crews were mostly Polish men flying twin-engined reconnaissance aircraft and when they took off, usually in fours, and were a safe distance out to sea, the rapid short burst of machine gun fire could be heard as the aircrews checked that the guns were in good operational order. They would then spread out and take up an assigned search area far out to sea. When the planes were not in use they were parked under trees across from the main road. In fact when the planes arrived or departed from this area by means of towing, the main road was closed off momentarily to stop the traffic.

In 1942 my cousin Ernie Cairns and I went on a visit by tandem to Ballyhalbert and we were able to stop and watch the airfield without hindrance. We were lucky to be there when planes were returning from patrol. To this day the remains of the steel tubes and concrete bases of the beacons can be seen at low tide.

A short distance along the sea front at Ballyhalbert is a safe little sheltered harbour. I never saw much use being made of this and often wondered if this was because it dried out when the tide receded, rendering it unsuitable for normal boating activity. For years in the early 1950s a strange craft was anchored in the harbour. It was of very strong steel construction, long and narrow in shape and not at all like the conventional design of boat. It was completely sealed all round on the outside except for a trap door which allowed access inside.

I often walked out to see it at low tide and was told that a chap had actually submerged in the craft but was brought to the surface with a great deal of difficulty. After lying unused in the harbour for a great many years it was next seen at anchor in Portavogie harbour. I later found out that this was built by a local man called Smith who owned quarries at Antrim. There were canals leading to the quarries and the boat was to be used for transporting the dynamite to the quarries.

Adjacent to Ballyhalbert harbour on the right is a gate which allowed access to rough terrain which was about 15 feet high above the shore line. This led further round to Coastguard houses. These houses had a link road round to Portavogie. In the area between the gate and coastguard houses, almost a quarter of a mile separated the mainland from Burial Island.

The name Burial Island, I was told, was given to these grass covered rocks out in the sea because, in historical times, when the Danes plundered the coast here, they used this area as a burial site for any of their men who died or were killed away from their homeland. They even brought Danish soil with them for this purpose.

m.v. 'ROSKVA'

Burial Island has been the scene of two shipwrecks in my lifetime. I previously swam out to this island in the early 1950's in a rubber suit but found nothing of interest. Then in 1955 a ship went aground here. She was a Norwegian diesel coaster called the m.v. 'ROSKVA' which was around 800 tons. She was holed but fortunately was refloated and beached at Ballyhalbert for repairs before being finally refloated in deep water. Because of the adverse weather conditions I was not able to swim out to the 'ROSKVA' and had to be content

M.V. "Roskva" aground at Burial Island, 1955.

with taking a photograph from the mainland. The strange thing was that this ship was to go aground again in July 1956 on Russell Rock, just off 'The Maidens' Lighthouse on the County Antrim coast but under a different name - the 'DOUGLAS'.

The 'WILLEMIGN'

August 1958 brought Burial Island into the news again with the wreck of the Dutch coaster 'WILLEMIGN' which was of similar size to the 'ROSKVA'.

The 'WILLEMIGN' went aground on the landward side of the island just south of Ballyhalbert Harbour. She had a cargo of fertilizer on board and was in danger of breaking in two when she was left high and dry at low tide. I travelled down on my L.E. VELOCETTE motor-bike, complete with diving suit, mask and fins etc. but with air bottle. This time I brought my camera.

On arrival at the grassy bank along the water's edge I was surprised at the number of sightseers who had already turned up. Because the wreck was on the landward side of the island facing the mainland, they had a grandstand view of the salvage preparations. I picked a quiet rocky gully and arranged my gear

"Willemign" aground at Burial Island, Co. Down, August 1958 (salvage ship in background).

Captain's bridge of ''Willemign'' aground at Burial Island, 1958.

on the turf. The tide was full in. So with my gear on I entered the cold water. I had my camera wrapped in a plastic bag and tucked safely against my chest inside the rubber suit. I enjoyed being carried along on the now outgoing tide. I could see workmen assembled on the deck over the hold. While one man operated the winch of the ship's crane which lowered a large hinged metal bucket down into the hold, another man guided the bucket on the cable from the crane to where other men were waiting ready with long shovels to load the fertilizer into it. The crane then deposited the contents of the bucket into the sea. Of course if the water level dropped to expose the bottom of the ship, operations were ceased immediately as there would have been no water to support the ship. While all this activity was in progress I observed the salvage ship at anchor seaward of the rocks.

The distance was much further than it looked and as I swam out I allowed the current to take me at a tangent to the grounded ship and then closed in near the stern. By now the workmen were aware of my presence and one of them indicated to his eyes and pointed to the bucket, warning me of the danger to my eyes with the dust of the jettisoned cargo of fertilizer which by now had mixed with the sea water making it a most vivid green colour. Taking the man's advice I put my mask over my eyes. I stayed some thirty feet away from the ship. I managed this by treading water (i.e. staying upright) in about 20 feet of water, working my flippers against the current. This enabled me to take the camera out of the plastic bag and take photographs of the operation. I re-wrapped the camera tightly again in the plastic bag and replaced it inside my rubber suit.

I then swam away from the stranded ship to clear the rocks as I had planned to swim to the highest part of Burial Island and have my lunch which was also tucked inside my rubber suit. It was then I had a frightening experience. I was still floating on my back in

"Willemign" — crew jettison cargo of fertiliser overboard, 1958.

20 feet of water when something large and heavy pushed strongly against my back.I immediately thought of a shark and turned round, at the same time grabbing my diving knife which was strapped round my leg for protection. I found it to be a very large jellyfish which the current had pushed in my direction. The offending jellyfish was deep red in colour and measured almost 30 inches in diameter while its feelers, each loaded with poison fluid, fanned out in the water to a depth of 3 feet.

I increased speed and drew ahead of the jellyfish but not before my left wrist was severely stung by some of its feelers. There had been a gap at my wrist where the arm of the rubber suit met the rubber glove. By this time I had been carried almost half a mile towards Portavogie and it took quite a bit of effort to get back against the current towards Burial Island again where I had my lunch and continued to watch the salvage operations.

I re-entered the cold water and approached my starting point from the outer side of the island landing in among the seaweed. Some of the sightseers came over to have a look at my gear. One young chap, who was a doctor, examined my wrist which by now was getting red and blotchy and was starting to ache. The doctor advised me to have it treated in hospital. I made my way home, happy at the thought of being able to take photographs. The jellyfish sting was to give me pain for about two weeks afterwards. I attended Templemore Day Hospital for treatment. While a creature of this size is dangerous to the unsuspecting swimmer, it does not purposely attack a person. It is completely at the mercy of tide and current for direction. I have encountered these jellyfish at a depth of 80 feet and even when dead the poison remains active for some time. Of course the much smaller transparent like jellyfish around our shores are quite harmless and can be held safely in the hand without any after effects.

Official Opening of Extension to Portavogie Harbour

One morning in the 1950s I cycled to Portavogie and purely by accident I was to witness a very interesting and moving ceremony. It was the official opening of the new extension to the harbour which had been extensively deepened and improved. The village of

Portavogie was all decked out in flags and bunting as were the fishing boats taking part in the ceremony. I left my bike on the rocks and found a good vantage point high up where I could see over the inner harbours and right out to sea. At the entrance to the outer harbour was a table stacked with books which appeared to be Bibles and ladies were busy unpacking more of these. From where I was sitting I could see everything that was going on.

The inner harbours were packed with fishing boats and the music of bands could be heard in the background. Hundreds of people had come out to see the spectacle. The vessels proceeded in line to sail out of the inner harbours. On the main harbour wall at one of the steel accommodation ladders a lady was positioned about halfway down. She was supported by a man on the opposite side of the ladder who was obviously there to ensure she did not fall. As each vessel approached this accommodation ladder the skipper leaned over the side and was presented by the lady with a Bible, followed by a handshake. There was also another lady positioned at the top of the ladder who kept replenishing the Bibles from a large pile. It took about two hours for the inner harbours to empty. Each vessel, on receiving its Bible, proceeded about half a mile out in deep water where they anchored side by side in a horizontal line facing the land. A large newly painted and bedecked boat with dignitaries on board passed the line of ships and as it passed each one, the crew of that particular vessel would send up cheers as if in a salute. After the ceremony all the vessels dispersed back to their moorings in the harbour and the crowds congregated on board and around the boats. I was thrilled to be there and have the privilege of seeing such an impressive and touching ceremony. I cycled on to Portaferry and then home to Belfast after a memorable day.

'FRIDA BLOKZUL'

A road winds from Portavogie past Quinton Castle and along the shoreline via a little branch road to Kearney Point. Late one evening in March 1962 while listening to the radio I heard on the News Bulletin that a ship had run aground there. So at 5.00 a.m. the next morning I travelled from Belfast on my L.E. VELOCETTE motor-

''Frida Blokzul'' aground at Kearney Point, 1962.

Left to right — Crew Protection Member George Calvert along with James Gowan and Sammy Anderson — in wheelhouse of "Frida Blokzul", 1962.

"Frida Blokzul", 1962.

"Frida Blokzul," 1962.

"Frida Blokzul," Kearney Point, 1962.

Noel on left at "Frida Blokzul," 1962.

bike. On arriving at Kearney Point the ship was not hard to find. She had run aground on a very high tide. In fact one of my photographs shows her high and dry adjacent to a gate in one of the fields.

As I was walking around the ship in the early hours of the morning the crew protection member invited me aboard dropping a flexible steel ladder for me to climb. So armed with my camera I climbed up and had a conversation with the three men on board. It was the Protection Crew Member's job to look after and guard the ship while she was aground. I was shown round the stranded ship and allowed to take photographs. The men were extremely interested in 'Ticking Annie,' the remote control clockwork timer fitted to the camera.

I took photographs of the men and promised to post them copies. They gave me their addresses and, as promised, I posted photos to them at a later date.

''Frida Blokzul, Kearney Point, 1962.

I visited the ship two weeks later and a lot of preparation had been put in hand. Sharp rocks had been broken down and a pathway blasted across the rocks to deep water. Meanwhile a concrete ramp was built under the ship for a length of about 100 feet straight out to sea. Along the concrete runway was embedded a length of standard railway line which led out to deep water. A strong steel pulley wheel with steel side sheets was welded at the ship's bow to engage the length of single railway line. To complete the project, steel rods were concreted in at a given distance on each side of the rail with flags on top so that when the tide was in, a steel flag lined pathway provided a safe channel to deep water. All was ready for the re-float attempt which would take place at a very high tide with little or no wind. When I revisited the same site a year later the ramp going out to deep water could still be seen.

The Routen Wheel

The road now leads from Kearney towards Portaferry. Another interesting thing to look out for is the ROUTEN WHEEL whirlpool which is about half a mile before the harbour where the Strangford Ferry berths. The terrain here which follows the waters edge round in a curve, is a bit rough and heavy going, and is quite muddy in parts. It is advisable to take an old pair of shoes or wellies for this particular stretch and safer not to take children. After climbing the rocks in this area a small bay is approached and there is a good view of the whirlpool from this point as it is high up looking down into the bay close to the land. The best time to see this spectacle is in between high and low tides. At high tide the path can be inaccessible for a short time but it is only a brief period of approximately 15 minutes before it recedes. At high tide the whirlpool area appears to be quite tranquil but when the tide is either ebbing or flowing then the water is transformed into a dangerous swirling whirlpool. When at its peak, the energy spinning around is quite alarming and the water takes the form of a circular hole sucking downwards with a disturbing sound. The circular disturbance around the hole can be up to 15 feet in diameter with secondary tidal disturbances in the vicinity. Certainly this is no place for swimmers or small boats!

Wartime Aluminium Lifeboat

Halfway between the whirlpool and Portaferry Harbour was beached a strange aluminium boat which I last saw about 1950. This boat had a very interesting history. It was one of a large number built as a specialised type of lifeboat for service in the Second World War. It was about 20 feet long with a 6-ft beam and resembled a conventional lifeboat in shape except that it was all covered in on the top but with hinged trap doors allowing access inside.

These boats were mainly used outside the normal range of land based rescue craft. They were carried underneath the fuselage of large bombers and were taken to remote areas far out from land in the North Atlantic ocean where boats would have been torpedoed. They had enormous parachutes attached to them and were dropped from a great height over the stricken area. After hitting the water the boat would remain floating allowing survivors from the torpedoed ships to climb up the strong netting which was strung around the sides and gain entrance through the hinged doors at the top. The boat would then remain floating with the survivors safely inside protected from the cold elements and with emergency rations to help them stay alive until such times as rescue operations were effected. The chance of survival in an open lifeboat was very slim especially in winter but because of the design of these aluminium boats, many more lives were saved. These lifeboats were very much sought after by boating enthusiasts after the war who adapted them to suit their individual requirements.

I happened to mention about the one which I had seen during conversation in a boating club and by coincidence one of the men in the company was the actual owner. He was quite surprised but pleased that I had recognised it and knew of its former purpose.

Strangford Motor Boat

In the 1950s two of my friends and I were practising long distance cycling runs for our planned tour the following year down through England. This particular day we cycled from Belfast through Comber, Killyleagh and on to Strangford town, arriving there very late at night. We went to the quay to catch the motor-boat ferry to Portaferry but it was not in sight. While we were discussing what to do, a

Earlier type motor-boat used on the Strangford/Portaferry run in the 1950s.

woman came out of the ferryman's dwelling and when she realised we wanted to get across she told us to wait while she went back to the house. She came back with a lantern and started to signal in the darkness to her husband on the far side. He signalled back and she told us he was on his way over. Of course in those days there was just the one Strangford Ferry — a motor boat owned and operated by one man and two landing craft used to take vehicles across. It was a standard type motor boat unlike the larger and more luxurious car ferries operating this stretch today.

The motor-boat arrived and the ferryman seemed pleased that there were three of us plus our bicycles. Luckily it was a calm night with no rain as there was no shelter in the open boat. We arrived safely on the other side at Portaferry to continue our journey home by the long route.

Some years later an ex-army landing craft was the scene of a tragedy on this stretch of dangerous water. A lorry was being taken across with the driver and his passenger seated in the cab when the boat capsized and sank and one of them was drowned. This operation was ceased immediately and it was shortly after in 1969 that the modern purpose built car ferries were introduced on this short run. As a matter of interest the single fare for passengers on the open motor-boat was sixpence per person and a smaller charge for a bicycle.

Chapter 7
THE INNER SIDE OF STRANGFORD LOUGH

John Lee — Shipbreakers

About two miles north of Portaferry town there was a sheltered bay which was used by the firm of John Lee as a shipbreaking area. This was always of great interest to me especially during the period 1947 to 1959 as ships of various types were broken up here for scrap. My most memorable among these was a German submarine of the smaller coastal type. I cycled from Belfast several times down to this little bay to have the chance of seeing for myself at closer quarters the shipbreakers' progress in drawing the heavy submarine nearer to the beach. When they removed more material from the forward section, this was my chance to climb on to it one day when the workmen had left after their day's work. Having previously been inside a British submarine in Belfast, this stood me in good stead on this particular occasion as I found the German craft to be very similar in construction.

Since all the deck hatches were closed I had to enter by climbing up an iron ladder and down through the circular hatch in the coning tower and, with only my bicycle lamp for illumination, down through a further hatch which descended vertically into the dark interior of the submarine. It was quite slippery inside. This had been brought about by the submarine being purposely holed by the salvage crew to prevent it floating on incoming tides. Ship machinery is oily at the best of times and when the water level rose on each incoming tide this caused a thin film of oil to spread throughout the interior of the submarine. Also the smell of diesel was quite overpowering.

I walked slowly forward until I came to the torpedo tubes, the doors of which were in the 'closed' position. I tried to decipher the German instructions on how to operate them but did not make much headway. As I made my way back I passed the place where the torpedoes would have actually been stored on semi-circular racks. Between these racks and the coning tower was the first section of crew accommodation. I was intrigued by the hinged bunks with pull-across canvas awnings which would have shielded sleeping crew members from the bright intense lighting inside the submarine. It was hard to visualize how bright it would have been when all I had was a torchlight in utter darkness. As I came nearer to the coning tower I went into the chartroom which was devoid of charts or maps but had a few small tables in it as well as Officers' bunks on either side. I walked further along and through a bulkhead door which led into additional crew accommodation. As I walked on I then stepped into water which I did not see in the dark and this prevented me from going any further to examine the diesel engine and electric motor which powered the submarine. At this point I made my way back to the coning tower, climbing up through the two hatches and out of the submarine into broad daylight.

Several very valuable articles such as the periscope and an early type of computer for calculating the torpedo run had been removed and were lying on the dry beach nearby. They had been stripped of their most vital and precious optics and computer components. Because of the incoming tide I had just time for a quick scout round before heading back for home on my push-bike. I was severely reprimanded by my mother when I got home for the oily state of my clothes. I again visited the submarine some weeks later but by then, apart from the periscope, very few identifiable parts remained.

Another interesting craft which had been brought in for breaking up about the same time was a large tugboat of very unusual design. This was similar to photographs I had seen, of such craft used on the Mississippi to tow a fleet of heavily laden barges. The tug had two parallel funnels situated side by side rather than the more conventional design of one behind the other, but the strangest thing of all was the hull which was of wooden construction.

I would have liked to have swum out to this wreck as it lay in the sheltered bay but there was a lot of fuel oil leaking from it and floating on the surface of the water. When I visited the site much later the tugboat was in very poor condition and partly sunk. It appeared to be abandoned. Near the Mississippi-like craft was another unusual one for breaking up. She was named the

'LENASHIP' and was about 60 feet long and seemed to me to be of foreign construction. It had the appearance of a powerful tugboat and was unique in that it was mostly constructed of wood. It had a single tall mast and the bridge was curved in shape unlike the more usual square design.

Very strong steel beams, which seemed to be used for towing purposes, were fitted across the rear of the hull at the top about three feet above the deck. The craft appeared to have been powered by diesel engines. There was not much salvage to be had from this particular craft with the exception of its engines and it eventually sank and was broken up by sea action alone.

Luckily I took a photograph of the 'LENASHIP' but to do this I had to climb up the gantry of the demolition crane nearby. This particular crane itself was showing signs of wear and was also in a dilapidated condition. However from my vantage point I had an excellent panoramic view of the partly sunken wreck down below.

In the next small bay around from the one used by John Lee, was the remains of a steam fishing trawler which previously was moored at Ballydorn when it then had its funnel and wheelhouse intact.

The "Lenaship," late 1940s.

The scant remains of this particular vessel as it then lay in the bay consisted of the hull complete with wrought iron propeller but devoid of wheelhouse, decking and steam engine. This particular vessel was registered in the Isle-of-Man where a lot of similar fishing trawlers were then based. They were also once a familiar sight around the British Isles with their distinctive tall funnel and single mast. At high tide this wreck was always a popular site for skin divers. In fact I dived there myself. It was always a haven for small fish when the tide was in.

Opposite this little bay across the road was a house which had a whalebone arch positioned outside. This was a genuine whalebone and stood about 15 feet high. The width of the arch was about 12 feet. It was a familiar site there for many years and only in recent years has been removed.

"Dido-C" at Kircubbin, 1956.

"Dido-C" at Kircubbin, 1956.

'DIDO-C'

On round to Kircubbin and there in the little harbour could be seen the scant remains of an old wooden Swedish built craft. The name of this craft was 'DIDO-C'. This ship was previously anchored off the little harbour at Ringneil not far from the ruins of Nendrum Abbey. She was in very poor condition and for many years I gazed out at her lying there in the water. She was then moved across to Kircubbin and after a few years there, it seemed she was to have a new lease of life when the wheelhouse and decking were rebuilt. The large engine had been removed for overhaul. Sadly, however the re-building did not continue and the 'DIDO-C' once more lay abandoned until finally it was towed away from the jetty. It was then set on fire and allowed to burn to the waterline.

Swans Feeding

Working my way up the inside of Strangford Lough past Greyabbey and on to the Mountstewart area. Here at the mud flats one particular day I enjoyed a novel way of observing the wild swans feeding in the shallow waters of the lough. Wearing my rubber diving suit complete with face mask, snorkel and fins but without the air bottle, I entered the water some distance away from the feeding swans. Lying in the water head down I allowed the current to carry me slowly in the direction of the swans. Using my fins for propulsion I slowly drifted along towards them. As I thought, the birds were too busy feeding to pay any attention to me. I submerged a few times and the close up underwater view of the swans was quite fantastic. They submerged with wings retracted and their broad webbed feet seemed to force their bodies downward. I was so close I could see tiny bubbles coming from their nostrils as they snapped at the eel grass underneath the water. They were able to consume several beakfuls of the eel grass before propelling themselves to the surface for air. I thought it odd that while on the surface the swans dipped their beaks repeatedly into the water as if to wash down the eel grass. The current swept me gradually further away from the birds and when I was a reasonable distance to prevent them being alarmed I headed again for the shore. I had the pleasure of seeing shoals of almost transparent looking little fry swimming under my body. These tiny fish were not in the least frightened by my presence. The lough is extremely pleasant to explore in all its moods either in a boat or by walking along the shore. What never failed to excite me was when I snorkelled horizontally and was able to view at water level all around, especially in the late evening when the lengthening shadows gave depth of field to the sparkling ripples of water. I recall in 1948 being in the vicinity of Mountstewart along the shore. It was low tide on this particular occasion and I was able to walk along the sand flats to a little island which at high tide would be surrounded by water. I suddenly saw movement under my feet and noticed on the stony covered surface, tiny chicks emerging from eggs laid among the warm shingle, while above me swooped the parent birds trying to guard their chicks. These parent birds seemed to be quite different from the ordinary seagull. They were lightly speckled in colour and had sharp pointed wings. I was quite surprised to witness this scene as I had never seen chicks born on a beach before. I retraced my steps very carefully in order to avoid injuring any of the little chicks and made my way back to the mainland.

Conningburn

A short distance from here on the shores of Strangford Lough a little stream called Conningburn passed under the main road and into the lough. I recall in the late 1940s seeing here two wooden bathing huts which were in quite good condition and in fact on one occasion I sheltered in one of them from the rain. They were on stilts about three feet from ground level with wooden steps up to them. This must have been a popular bathing spot in earlier times. Across the road from these bathing boxes were the ruins of a water mill which, during its working life, was powered from the little burn by means of a man made waterfall.

Most of the machinery was gone and all that remained was the mainshaft and the skeletal remains of the water wheel.

While examining the remains of the water wheel I noticed bricks supporting the main bearing. On one of these bricks I was able to read the name CASTLE ESPIE quite clearly. I was quite pleased at seeing this brick as the Castle Espie brickworks which lay on the opposite side of the lough were also in ruins. It was the first and only time I personally had come across a named brick from this particular brickworks and I took a photograph of it.

Waterwheel gears at Conningburn, 1948.

Remains of waterwheel main drive shaft at Conningburn, 1950s.

Brick in main waterwheel bearing unit with Castle Espie on it, 1949.

Chapter 8

THE LEAD MINES AND FURTHER INLAND

The Lead Mines — Conlig

I was a constant visitor on my bicycle to the Lead Mines around the late 1940s/early 1950s. They always held a fascination for me. Here I usually ended up at the deep open mineshaft. Although barbed wire surrounded the shaft which was a very dangerous area to approach, I did manage once to lie down and lean over to enable me to see some way down the shaft which I estimated to be at least 150 feet deep and 10 feet square. Like another shaft some 200 yards away, it also had the scant remains of a wooden floor about 50 feet down. I wondered if this had been an earlier attempt to sheet in the dangerous hole. I was amazed on one occasion to watch a little robin fly down the shaft and land on a ledge there where it probably had a nest.

Because of my interest at that time in potholing I decided to explore for holes in the ground. I searched around and found what I presumed was a ventilation shaft about 50 yards over towards the second mine shaft which was in the direction of Helen's Tower. This may have served both mine shafts as an air vent. The descent into this vent was extremely rough. It was only the width of a human body and was almost vertical in places which made it difficult to hold myself from falling. I had to give up when I was only about 15 to 20 feet below the surface. I did notice that a flow of air was coming up and it smelt quite fresh. I had previously found an air vent at Castleward near Strangford which was only 100 yards from the main mineshaft there which is now filled in. I presume it must have been the practice to sink a secondary hole close to main access mineshafts.

One night in 1949 I cycled down to visit friends Jack Cairns and family who actually resided above the mines at Conlig in the vicinity of Whitespots in what was known as McNulty's house. In later years

Lead Mines with McNulty's house on the right, 1948.

this house was partly demolished but ruins can still be seen to this day.

At that particular time I was interested in radio crystal sets and wanted to use a lead crystal from these mines at Conlig. The sons of the family took me out in the darkness towards the mines. At a certain point they told me to wait while they went on. They returned in about 15 minutes with a handful of beautiful lead crystals which they actually found in the dark. These crystals gave me years of service with very good radio reception.

Also at Conlig lead mines on the right hand side of Whitespots was the McBurney Shaft and to the right of it again was the old Conlig shaft which, although in ruins, still had its engine house mostly intact and large sections of the machinery and cable structure remained inside. This shaft was partly hidden from view by thick undergrowth. I did a hair-raising feat here which now sends cold shivers down my spine when I think of the dangers involved plus the fact that I was on my own on this occasion.

I went down this shaft with a long length of rope. I looked around and near the entrance to the shaft I saw a vertical steel rod sticking out of the ground. I tied the rope securely to this steel rod and dropped the rest down the shaft. I then descended into the shaft by lowering myself down on the rope. I went down as far as a man made ledge which was about 15 feet down. I found that by lying on my tummy on this ledge and holding on to the rope, I could see about 50 feet vertically down into the shaft to a wooden platform covered with rubble. One side had fallen away and the mineshaft seemed to continue further down into the blackness. On dropping stones through the gap I could hear them falling quite a distance before landing on dry bottom. The sides of the shaft were extremely clean and seemed in very good order. I wondered why the platform was built across the deep shaft so far below the surface.

The stone built engine house was situated immediately above but to one side of the shaft entrance. It was devoid of all its internal fittings and even the floor had been removed. A semi-oval opening in the tall side of the engine house which faced the vertical drop of the shaft, had allowed the cables to enter the winding drum. At one side of the opening I was fascinated to find a deep groove which had been caused by the winding cable coming out of line and fouling the stonework during the time of its working life. This defect had been caused by the driveshaft falling out of alignment

The Lead Mines, Conlig, 1948.

Remains of engine house, Conlig Lead Mines, 1949.

and the steel cable rubbing against the stonework whilst in operation. Only a small section of the tiled roof of the engine house remained.

The area adjacent to this mineshaft was extremely hazardous in that large objects such as winding drums, axles, gearing etc., had been removed leaving holes in the ground up to five feet deep hidden by the long grass.

The ruins of the windmill at the Leadmines were also still quite impressive. The circular wall was wide at the base and slightly tapered to the top. The cap of the windmill and the blades were missing. As in conventional windmills the doorway was at the base. I suspected that the purpose of the windmill was either to pump water out of the shafts or to pump air into them or perhaps even to crush the stone to extract the lead ore.

On one particular visit on the approach to the quarry below the mines, I was walking across the council tip area and was amazed to see three vintage vacuum cleaners each operated manually and powered by hand bellows. All three were in excellent condition and would have been worth preserving. A few miles on in Clandeboye Estate is Helen's Tower a well known landmark in the area.

Helen's Tower

One day in 1948 I drove relations of mine to Helen's Tower on a visit to the caretaker family called Bruce. I was delighted to be allowed the opportunity of exploring the rooms in it. As I ascended the narrow stone stairway the walls were adorned with large metal plaques depicting different Coats of Arms. On turning these plaques over I was amazed and fascinated when I discovered each of them had been inscribed by American Troops stationed in Northern Ireland just prior to being transported to the battlefields of Europe in the Second World War. These inscriptions were hand written and mostly of a very personal nature giving their names, addresses and in some cases poems and personal messages which I found rather touching. It was sad to think some of the lads who inscribed these messages probably never saw their homeland again. Members of the Ulster Division were encamped in the grounds at Clandeboye and trained and drilled on the plain below Helen's Tower.

I went inside a couple of the rooms which were Gothic in style. They were partially furnished and quite musty. The top floor which was octagonal in shape had metal plates screwed to the walls. These plates had poems engraved on them by famous personalties such as Tennyson, Kipling and Browning. I then continued up to the roof of the tower and gained access through a door to the bastion outside. Here there was a raised wall all round and I was able to look over the tops of the trees in the forest below. I could actually spot birds' nests in the top branches of the trees. From this vantage point I could see part of the City of Belfast, the Holywood Hills, Belfast Lough and even further away the Antrim Hills including Slemish mountain. I could also see Scotland in the distance while in the immediate foreground was the County Down coastline with the Copeland Islands offshore. I finally returned to the ground floor of the tower and with my two relations enjoyed a homely cup of tea and cakes supplied by Mr and Mrs Bruce in their private quarters on the ground floor, before leaving again for home.

The building of Helen's Tower commenced in 1841 and was completed about 1850. Frederick Temple Hamilton BLACKWOOD erected it in memory of his mother Helen Selina.

A tower of similar design was built at Thiepval, Northern France about 1920 as a tribute to the sons of Ulster who died in the Battle of the Somme during the First World War 1914-1918. This second tower was paid for by public subscription from the people of Northern Ireland.

Rats in the Trees

One cold dark Autumn night in the early 1950s I was cycling home to Belfast after visiting friends near Donaghadee. On approaching Movilla I got off my bicycle to walk some of the steep hills. As I was walking the bicycle past some dense bushes I was aware of movement in the branches above me. I set the bicycle down to investigate and removing the bicycle lamp I directed the beam of light above me in the direction of the noise. To my amazement I saw lots of rats clutching the spindly branches and holding on with their little legs wrapped round them. This spectacle took me by surprise as I had never imagined rats could climb vertical branches. I continued to watch and it was obvious the rats held no fear of me so moving closer I could see they were eating the haws berries on the trees. It was an education to see how they balanced themselves and used their mouths to pick the berries, discarding the seeds as they were eating. I advanced further into the thicket and observed more of these rodents enjoying the feast and holding on some two to three yards above the ground. I was disappointed at not having my camera on this occasion to record this most unique scene.

My First TV Aerial

On the old road from Newtownards to Dundonald which in the 1950s was then the main road, there stood a house on a hill adjacent to a quarry site. This house had a large television aerial. Of course this was at the time when television was just coming into Northern Ireland and I had recently bought one of the very early nine inch television sets. Although the actual screen was only nine inches it was encompassed by a very large standing cabinet and not at all like the streamline models of today with their large screens. There was not even a Television Station in Northern Ireland at that time and the reception was long range, the nearest TV Station being in

Wales. I had noticed this aerial on a previous occasion so I went back on my bicycle one day and made a quick drawing of it noting the approximate size of the structure and number of reflecting bars. The aerials then, like TV sets, were a lot more ungainly than those of today. When I arrived home I showed the drawing to my father and he made an aerial out of scrap metal. This enabled us to get our first black and white picture which in those days was a rare treat.

The Sheep in the Thicket

Another day also in the early 1950s I was cycling from Belfast to Portaferry by way of Newtownards. I had just approached the 'Old Mill' Boarding Kennels on the old road from Dundonald to Newtownards which has now been incorporated into a Restaurant and Gift Shop. On this particular day the sun was so hot I dismounted at a stream on the left hand side and had a refreshing drink of spring water. I walked the bicycle up the long hill, enjoying the pleasant surroundings. The whole grassed area here was amass with bluebells making it a very picturesque scene. For no apparent reason my attention was directed across the busy road to a steep bank. There seemed to be something drawing me to this bank. I locked my bicycle, crossed the road and climbed the steep slope. I had never been up there in my life before. The ground was very rough and dropped slightly into a gully on the far side then levelled out to less undulating ground which was completely out of sight from the main road.

On approaching an area of dense thorny bushes I discovered a sheep lying on its side and hopelessly trapped by its wool in the thorns. By the large amount of droppings it was obvious the poor animal had been trapped there for some time. Also, the grass had been eaten right down within reaching distance of the sheep's head. I raced back to my bicycle to obtain tools from my cycle bag and returned to the unfortunate sheep. It took quite some time to get it free as the thorny branches had embedded themselves into the thick wool. The sheep did not hinder me in any way as I painstakingly cut away parts of the heavy wool coat, separating it from the thicket. I then lifted it up on its feet. It started to nibble at the fresh green grass. I sat with it for about an hour until it gained some strength. When it seemed none the worse for its ordeal I returned to my bicycle and resumed my journey to Portaferry still puzzled by what invisible force had drawn me to that particular spot and to the plight of the sheep.

Chapter 9

CASTLE ESPIE AND ON TO CASTLE WARD

Castle Espie

On out now to the Mahee Island Road to Castle Espie. In 1950 the remains of the Castle Espie Brickworks previously mentioned, were in reasonable order and well worth visiting. I went down there quite regularly as I found the brick kiln quite fascinating.

The main oven was a tunnel of about 50 yards long and about 7 to 8 feet high. Inside the semi-circular roof the surface of the brick had been melted into a shiny glazed mass by the terrific heat of the furnace. At intervals along this oven were little projecting doorways some of which still had the dry bricks set in. At the time when the brickworks would have been in operation, bricks that were newly made and unbaked were stacked in rows in criss-cross fashion right along the whole length of the tunnel up to the curved ceiling. They were wheeled in through the projecting brick doorways probably on little trolleys or trucks. The dry bricks were placed temporarily in the doorways and the doorways sealed to prevent loss of heat. These dry bricks would then be in place until the inside ones were baked. All the bricks were then removed. These new bricks had the name 'CASTLE ESPIE' cast into them on the polished side. The dry bricks were used over and over again for sealing the doorways mentioned above. I tried on several occasions to find the source of heat for the brick kiln but was never able to positively identify it.

To the right hand side of the tunnel at the lough shore, a long stone jetty projected out into deep water. This provided source of shipment for the bricks. On one occasion when the kiln was in disuse I ventured into the dark tunnel and had to beat a hasty retreat when I was confronted by a bullock.

Between the kiln and the lough shore were two lakes or dams, one large and one small. The larger dam was further away from

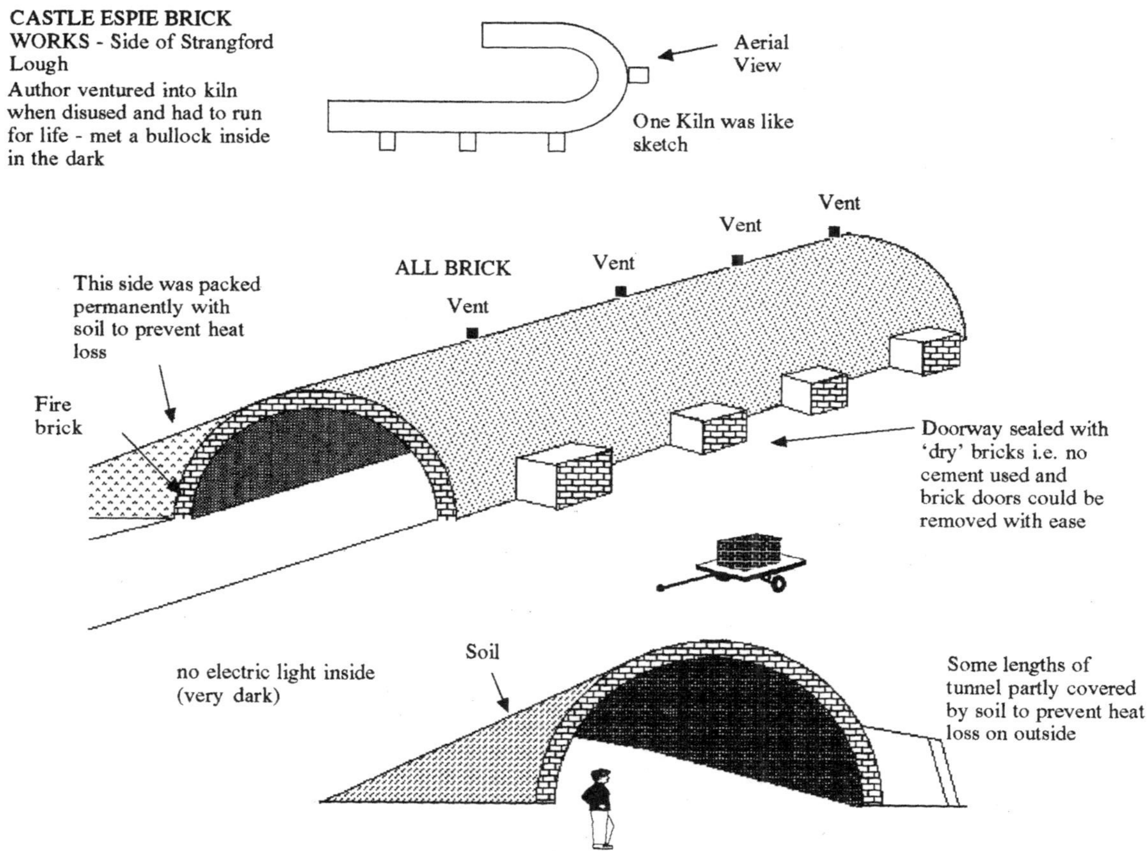

Diagram from memory of Brickworks Kiln, Castle Espie in 1950s.

the kiln and I had been told it had been the source of clay for the bricks but eventually the sea had penetrated the bank and flooded the workings. However in 1950 I dived into it using an aqua-lung. I found the visibility virtually nil because of brown sediment. About 15 to 20 feet down I encountered several large objects. I was able to feel a buggy wheel which I tried to turn but found it to be solid with rust. After colliding with a few more unknown objects I decided it was prudent to head again for the surface. A gentleman who had been watching me with interest, told me he had never seen an aqua-lung before and was very pleased when I let him inspect it more closely. In fact I even let him breathe through the mouthpiece and he was elated with the experience of breathing in the cold clean air. He told me there were spades and four-wheeled trucks lying at the bottom of that particular dam. While this dam was filled with salt water due to the sea seeping into it over the years through the clay side wall, the smaller dam still contained fresh water. I did not dive in this one as on previous occasions I had always found it to be a fruitless exercise in fresh water dams because of poor visibility.

Unfortunately in later years progress took its toll and the old brickworks complex was levelled out for the construction of a runway for a private aircraft landing strip.

Mahee Island

On to Mahee Island which now because of the addition of a man-made causeway is strictly no more an island. The road over the causeway passes adjacent to the ruins of Sketrick Castle which goes back to the 1400s. This castle although in very bad state of disrepair to the extent of being hazardous, had a unique feature on the ground floor of the inner room. This room has a 'murder hole' built into its roof. The purpose of this murder hole was for the inhabitants to retreat to the first floor in the event of the castle being besieged and pour boiling liquids down over any invaders trying to get access to the upper floors.

On a visit to the castle ruins in 1948 I entered the little doorway and then into a very dark inner room. My father was with me on this occasion and he returned to his 'BABY AUSTIN' car for paper and matches. Meanwhile I held my hands out and walked carefully

Ruins of Skettrick Castle, 1950.

around the dark room and back to the door which is several feet above the ground. My father had returned and handed me some lighted paper inside. When my eyes got accustomed to the bright light I was shocked by the sight of a large square hole in the centre of the room which I could easily have fallen into had I not stayed close to the surrounding wall. On returning to Sketrick Castle many years later I was relieved to see the hole was filled in with rubble. I often wondered for what purpose this hole was used which was at ground level below the murder hole previously mentioned.

Nendrum Abbey

Past Sketrick Castle is a short road to the right and about a hundred yards along access can be gained to the ruins of Nendrum Abbey, a tenth century monastic settlement. This has always been quite an impressive site but even more so since it was taken over by the National Trust as the grounds are now kept in first class order.

The Monastery proper would seem to have been relatively small. The side which faces the direction of the Lightship Clubhouse at Ballydorn has the scant remains of where various workshops such as metal and leather were sited. The large well, now dry, can also

Remains of Round Tower, Nendrum Abbey, 1990.

Noel showing Welsh visitors Bill and Marian Morgan part of ruins of Nendrum Abbey, 1990.

Marian and Bill examining another part of Nendrum ruins, 1990.

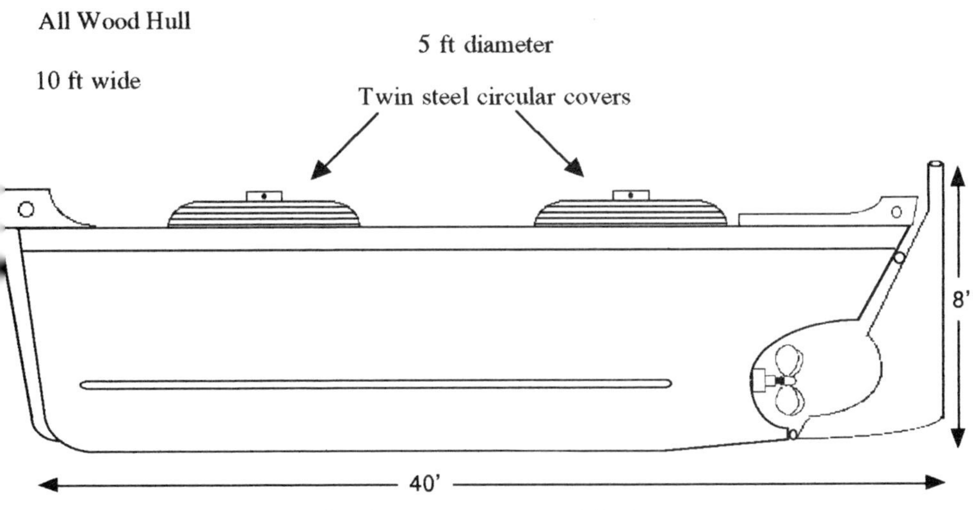

Sketch of mystery boat near Nendrum.

still be seen. The bell of this monastery which had been previously hidden to safeguard it from invaders, was discovered a long time afterwards and is now in the custody of the Ulster Museum at Stranmillis.

In 1947 at a little jetty near Nendrum Abbey a strange craft was tied up and I often wondered about its history. It was built of wood and had strong twin steel domed circular covers fitted into the deck. Each cover was about 8 feet in diameter. As I was unable to open these covers I never found out what was below deck.

The strongly built wooden hull was devoid of masts and although shaped to accommodate an engine I did not see any evidence of a propellor.

When passing by several years later there was no sign of the craft although I could see grooves in the mud caused by the weight of the hull. She had no name but faintly painted at the bow was W3.

Drummond Lathe

Another short road branching from Sketrick Castle to the left of the one to Nendrum leads finally to Mahee Island Golf Course but at the right hand side is a neat slipway and boathouse and here on a cold winter's day around 1949 I chanced to come across a very enterprising gentleman wearing a heavy overcoat and cap. He was operating a Drummond Round Bed lathe mounted on a strong wooden framework with twin wheels at one end and long handles at the other end but the most surprising thing to me was the large twin bladed propeller mounted above the lathe. This was connected by a large Vee belt which he used as a source of power. The long handles enabled it to be wheeled in and out of the garage on the slipway. As I watched he turned the frame round until the propeller started to turn by wind power. It revolved rapidly and in turn the chuck of the lathe was soon spinning at high speed. He manoeuvred the saddle which was the sliding framework holding the cutting tool and thus ensured the cutting tool was in proper contact with the workpiece. As the tool cut into the workpiece little clouds of burning oil smoke wafted away in the wind. After some minutes work he stepped down and lifted the trolley to one side so that the propeller was no longer receiving energy from the wind and the workpiece then came to a stop. He then released the chuck and

Robert Ardill Monument, 1971.

withdrew the newly machined material, fitting it to some apparatus he was building. He was using pieces of material from a scrapped motor car close at hand. I had a very interesting conversation with the gentleman as I myself had just served my apprenticeship as an ironturner in Harland & Wolff and was well acquainted with the working of a lathe, so we had a lot in common.

I retraced my steps for a few yards and came upon a private entrance which led to the bare lough shore. I worked my way across marshy ground to a round conical memorial. This monument stood about twenty feet high and had tiered steps partly round it. On one side it also had recessed stone steps leading to the top. These were about the width of one's body. At the base of the memorial was a name plate to Robert Ardill and about four feet from the ground was an oval door similar to a boiler inspection door. I visited this monument again in 1971 with my wife Rita and a friend Jean Stevenson.

It is possible that in more recent times this monument may be out of bounds because a bird sanctuary is now in the vicinity and permission may be required to visit it.

Kilmood Church

Back now to the road junction and past the premises of David Coey — Produce Merchant. A turning on the left here leads to Kilmood. When I visited Kilmood in 1950 the little church there was still intact. I had on this occasion visited the grave of 'Daft Eddy' mentioned in the book entitled 'Smugglers of Strangford Lough'. In more recent times a restaurant was built at Sketrick Island named after 'Daft Eddy'. On my way back I came again to Kilmood Church. I spoke to the Caretaker who brought me inside the church. The floor which had an iron grille-like catwalk was not at ground level. In fact when I looked down at the floor I saw grass growing about three feet below. Heating pipes ran along the length of the pews. This church has since been dismantled.

'PETREL' — Lightship Clubhouse for Down Cruising Club

From Kilmood Church the road twisted and turned in the direction of 'PETREL' the lightship which is permanently moored at Ballydorn and is the Club House of Down Cruising Club which incidentally is celebrating its 25th year (1993) on board 'PETREL'. It is named

"Petrel" Lightship Clubhouse for Down Cruising Club, 1969.

"Petrel" Lightship Clubhouse for Down Cruising Club, 1991.

after the petrel (web-footed sea bird). Quite a few lightships of the same design as 'PETREL' were moored in the vicinity of dangerous reefs around the Irish Coast. These have all been replaced by more modern technology.

In July 1991 a relation of mine from New Zealand, Andrew Beattie and his girlfriend Allison were over in Northern Ireland. They were quite impressed when my wife and I took them aboard 'PETREL'.

Long Distance Swim

In 1949 I cycled down from Belfast to Ballydorn on Strangford Lough and after leaving my bike with local people I changed into my 'dry' rubber diving suit. With this suit I wore a wide belt-like inflatable safety harness. Attached to the harness was a lifejacket which I made out of an ordinary inflatable rubber pillow. Inside this pillow I fitted a small carbon dioxide pressure cylinder about three inches long. By manually depressing a lever this caused a needle to puncture the cylinder seal thus releasing the high pressure of gas which in turn inflated the lifejacket by means of a non-return valve. This method would only be used in a critical situation as the small air cylinders were quite expensive to replace. If time was not an important factor a second inexpensive method of inflation could be carried out by blowing orally into a tubed mouthpiece also through a non-return valve. I had previously tried out this lifejacket in 30 feet of water off Blackhead using both methods. The cylinder method was more effective making me surface so quickly that my ears popped.

So complete with rubber fins and gloves I began a long swim from the little jetty at Ballydorn just at the site where the lightship is today now berthed. At that time in Ballydorn Bay there was a partly sunken steam trawler. I had to be careful not to get pushed against this wreck by the very swift outgoing current in case I ripped or damaged the rubber suit. Incidentally the remains of this steam trawler now lie in a small bay off Portaferry. The outgoing tide carried me out of 'The Dorn' and on towards Ringhaddy. I then took a short cut between two islands and stepped ashore at Long Sheelagh. This island is a long shaped mass of shingle and is almost covered at high tide. I had my packed lunch here which I had stuck down inside my rubber suit to keep it dry. I then headed down to Portaferry on the Kircubbin side of the lough, passing John Lee's ship dismantling yard. The water here was very much colder and I had to take care to avoid contact with the open type motor boats which served Portaferry and Strangford towns. These two motor boats were the forerunners of the present day Strangford ferry.

I rested for a while on rocks in among mud flats near the harbour and my outfit caused some stir among the locals, as in those days diving suits were a rare sight. This point was about ten miles from where I first set out at Ballydorn so I started out on my return journey. I had to exercise great caution approaching John Lees as some jagged lengths of steel projected out of the sea. I was spotted here by neighbours from Belfast who reported to my parents that they had seen me although they did not know I had swum all the way from Ballydorn. So word of my whereabouts had preceded my arrival home. I had to swim carefully past Kircubbin to avoid colliding with a number of lobster pots anchored here. The bright sun was now beginning to set low down in the sky and occasional yachts appeared heading towards Portaferry. On this particular occasion I did not encounter any fish which was unusual. I had to swim through lots of scum on the surface of the water between Kircubbin and Ballydorn. This caused a thick slime around the chest of my suit. As I approached Ballydorn once more the temperature of the water was warmer and once more attention was drawn by onlookers to my diving suit as I waded ashore after ten hours swimming in Strangford Lough. Before I left the water I rubbed most of the slime off my suit with wet sand and returned to the grounds of the cottage where I had left my bike. I changed out of my diving suit and cycled home.

Ringhaddy

One time while cycling along the main Killyleagh Road from Belfast, I decided to branch down to Ringhaddy. This was a very congested area with parked cars belonging to the boating fraternity. At the little harbour a track to the left led me to a wooded area on the lough side, past an old castle and just before the dilapidated ruins of a church were several tall trees. The efforts of an artist were etched on the trunks of two of these depicting a sailing ship in full rig typical of the multi-masted schooners of a bygone period. It must have taken many hours to accomplish this.

Paddy Menarey's Grave

Just across the water from these trees is Dunsy Island where there is a strange memorial consisting of boulders. On the top of these boulders is the skeleton of a sheep's skull. This marks the grave of Paddy Menarey who it was alleged, was murdered many years ago when returning to the island after winning money gambling on the mainland.

Lobster Claws

In 1972 I visited the island of Long Sheelagh in Strangford Lough early one morning in my dinghy. I had my dog with me on this particular occasion. It was about high tide and only the top mound was visible above the water. I beached the dinghy and walked along the top with the dog. The dog started barking at something in the seaweed. On investigating I discovered a large lobster in the seaweed and on lifting it I realised it was dying. I carefully enclosed it in a circle of rocks on the mound and left it to die in peace. I returned to Long Sheelagh a week later and found that the lobster had died. I removed the large claws or pincers. One of pincers was much larger than the other. When I returned home I preserved them and mounted them on a plaque. I took the plaque to Queen's University where I worked, and after the experts had examined them, they were of the opinion that the lobster had been twenty three years old, so it had enjoyed a long life in Strangford Lough. I still have these lobster claws at home to this day.

Pike Stone

On the main road between Killyleagh and the Quoile area is the famous pike stone which was used to sharpen the pikes in the times of the renowned historical battle of Ballynahinch as detailed in the book 'BETSY GREY or HEARTS OF DOWN'. On the odd occasion in the past I have seen the portrait of King Billy painted on the stone.

The Quoile

About a mile past the pike stone my friend Billy Rodgers and his son Ronnie took me one day to a water-logged inlet of the Quoile. We went over some very wet and marshy ground to a spot where there was growing in abundance luscious looking green watercress. We each picked a bunch of this watercress to take to our homes.

The Quoile river today is now a very quiet, tranquil and scenic area since the barrier was built across the tidal section. The quay now deserted was once a hive of activity being used by large sailing craft for discharging coal. The scant remains of one such ship can still be seen high and dry to the right hand side of the quay.

The 'ARETHUSA'

A familiar sight at the mooring across from this quay in the centre of the then tidal estuary in the 1950s was the unusual passenger vessel the 'ARETHUSA'. This vessel was double decked. The lower deck had large windows while the upper deck was used by passengers for sunbathing in good weather. It was also protected at the edges by square steel grilles for the safety of the passengers. From this deck, because of its height above the water line which was about twelve feet, a magnificent view could be had in all directions.

When the Quoile barrier was built years later, all the boats had to vacate this area and the 'ARETHUSA' which had been a most popular tourist attraction in Strangford Lough was towed to Carrickfergus escorted by a flotilla of small craft. I saw her in Carrickfergus some years later but was sad to find her partly submerged and dismantled. She was a sorry sight with water flowing through her once luxurious interior.

Castleward

In the late 1940s I cycled down to Castleward and through a big open driveway off the main road. I had not realised at this time that I was entering private property and I ended up at the main door of the large house. I dismounted from my bicycle and approached an elderly lady who was seated in the doorway in a large ornate wicker chair which was closed in around the sides. I apologised profusely for trespassing. She was very courteous and immediately put me at my ease. She was clad in a very long dark dress which billowed down to the ground. She had a shawl round her shoulders and wore a tightly fitted crocheted bonnet. In her lap lay a piece of colourful tapestry in a frame which she had set aside when talking to me. She was very interested in my push bike. I observed behind her large chair the stuffed figure of a large free standing brown bear in the porch. When I showed interest in it she allowed me to go behind her to inspect the bear. She had a name for it but I cannot remember what it was. After having had a pleasant conversation with the charming lady I took my leave and followed her advice by leaving the estate by way of the lead mines which was a less private route out of the estate. I found out later that the charming lady was in fact Lord Bangor's mother. Lord Bangor who had resided at Castleward died in 1950 and was buried at sea. The motor boat containing his leaded coffin left the jetty at Castleward on 20 November 1950 and the coffin was released into the water. I returned to Castleward many years later when it was owned by the National Trust and open to the public. I explored the mines there and found the main shaft over in the direction of Audley's Castle close by. The square shaft was partly filled in with huge boulders almost to ground level. I discovered over to the right hand side of the main shaft on top of raised ground the remains of narrow twin shafts, one of which was exuding fresh air. These twin shafts may have been exploratory holes for the main shaft. On looking to the left of the main shaft towards the shore line I came upon an old thick stone built box with a strong lockable door which I presumed was used to house the explosives for the working of the mine. The lock was off the door and I was able to look inside. I found it to be quite empty but clean and dry. It is still possible to pick up pieces of lead ore scattered about here. I was greatly disappointed at not being able to go down into the actual mine itself. I wondered if the workings had been in good order and if, because of its proximity, the seams actually extended under the sea. The little jetty had the remains of a small crane which was probably used for loading the lead ore aboard the sailing ships. The mines during their working life had been a source of wealth to the estate.

In August 1976 my wife and I spent a very pleasant two weeks in our small sixteen foot cabin cruiser moored off this jetty at Castleward. There was a sunken wreck positioned out from the edge of the shore which was completely covered by water except at low tide when it was just barely visible.

At low tides during the mornings and afternoons, I rowed over to the wreck and waited till the tide receded enough to allow me to stand on the exposed remains. I paced out in steps where the deck house would have been and started digging. I was able to clear quite an area before the approaching tide forced me aboard the dinghy again. On the third day I penetrated the cabin area and in the remains of this I unearthed an antique glass-ridged bottle with the damaged delph figure of a highlander and a ship's pulley block. The rising tides each day prevented me from penetrating any deeper and I had to abandon any further attempt. During this time we were able to explore the beautiful house, gardens and grounds of Castleward. The house itself is unique in that it combines two

Noel beside stuffed bear at Castle Ward, 1990.

different styles of architecture. This was the result of husband and wife favouring their own styles so they compromised. The husband chose the Classical style while his wife chose Gothic and so the house on one side is in Classical style while the other side is in Gothic style. Admission can be gained into the house for a moderate charge. Inside the two styles are further in evidence with double doors of each style in the rooms. The stuffed bear was still on display inside. In fact as recently as 1990 I had my photograph taken beside it.

There is a Victorian laundry in the courtyard and at certain times during the tourist season demonstrations of Victorian laundering are re-enacted. There is also a very interesting tourist shop and very pleasant tea rooms with home baked produce. The sunken walled garden is quite beautiful and a pleasant walk takes one down by the lake and also over to Audley's Castle nearby. From the battlements of this castle one can enjoy a magnificent view over the lough. Truly this is quite a lovely spot.

Chapter 10

BALLYNAHINCH AND ON TO NEWCASTLE

Ballynahinch

I cycled down here from Belfast on a pleasant day in 1951. I stopped to admire some deer grazing on the steep slopes of a big estate on the right hand side of the road. Further on from here on the left hand side was a watermill which was in very good order but unfortunately was not accessible to the public. I would have loved to have had a closer look at it. Branching right from here the road became very steep with narrow bends. I walked the bicycle for long periods along it. I passed under a tall stone decorative arch which spanned the road. There did not seem to be a specific purpose for this arch other than just being ornamental. I arrived at the famous 'Spa' which encompassed the derelict ruins of several stone buildings which in their heyday were renowned for the healing properties of the waters. This particular area had been used by the Army during the Second World War.

I walked through the different covered-in bath houses which were drained of water. Most of the doors and windows were broken. I came to the pump house and tried to work the pump lever but it did not appear to be connected to the pump diaphragm. I came across several badly bashed army issue tin hats lying around. I stood there trying to visualise what the original grandeur of this place would have been like and thought how sad it was to see it in its present abandoned state. A short distance away on the opposite side of 'The Spa' was the remains of a well built maze of puzzle paths comprising dense hedging of about six foot high with large bare patches through it. I tried to wend my way through the maze but did not make much progress and as I was getting a bit pressed for time with a long cycle run home in front of me, I decided like others before me to cheat and take a short cut by escaping through the sides of some of the sparse sections of it.

Temple 100 Motor Cycle Race 1949

I left home on my push bike early one morning in 1949 to cycle to The Temple, a small village on the Ballynahinch to Newcastle road in the vicinity of Saintfield. On this occasion I went to see the motor cycle race which was being held that day. It was essential to make an early start as the roads were to be closed off before the race. The morning was dry but overcast and I enjoyed the run down even though the traffic on the roads was quite heavy.

I arrived in time to get a good vantage point which was about 50 yards from the start of the race. The first competitor was flagged off and as he was passing on the opposite side to where I was standing his engine failed and he had to pull in to the side. I felt so sorry for him breaking down so soon. One of the marshals came to his aid and changed the sparking plug, enabling him to continue in the race to cheers of encouragement from the crowd.

One of the spectators who was sitting on a porch roof of one of the houses got so excited he partly slid off the edge of the roof and had to be pulled back up by his friends. This was just minutes after I had taken the photograph. This year 1993 the Temple Motor Cycle Race celebrated its centenary — 100 years old.

Competitor in Temple Motor Cycle Race, 1949.

Spectators at Temple Motor Cycle Race, 1949. Notice man seated on porch roof.

Ballynoe Stone Circle

Another place which held a great fascination for me was Ballynoe Stone Circle which I visited in 1949. This is one of the finest examples of megalithic structures in Northern Ireland going back to 2000 BC. It is situated roughly between Downpatrick and Ballykinlar in the vicinity of Ballynoe Railway Station. Ballynoe Stone Circle was quite a tourist attraction being Ulster's smaller version of Stonehenge with its huge boulders, some of them 7 feet in height, in circular formation. The farmer had conveniently swathed a track through the hay right round the site for the convenience of visitors. After enjoying this very ancient link with the past I made my way back to the little country road and about a quarter of a mile away I came upon a small building which was used as a school house come Gospel Hall. While cycling past this hall I got a whiff of carbide gas. I dismounted from my bicycle and went back to the little hall to investigate. I found there an acetylene gas generator which was housed outside at the end of the hall. Copper pipes led from this generator to a number of gas lamps inside the hall. These gas lamps did not require any form of mantel because of the cleanliness and brightness from the carbide gas. The operation of these carbide lamps was by means of the top section containing a quantity of fresh water which was controlled by a serrated valve releasing as required, a constant drip of water. This water in turn penetrated the lower chamber of the lamp which was filled with carbide stones held down by a retaining wire spring. As the drops of water made contact with the stones, acetylene gas was generated and this produced an intense white light when ignited by the spark of the flint which was generated by a manual turn of the flint wheel. Once ignited the light was continuous until the carbide stones disintegrated into a white powder several hours later. The thing about the carbide was once the lamps were ignited they had to run their course until all the carbide was consumed as it would have been inappropriate to cut off the water supply, bearing in mind the carbide stones already dampened would still have continued to generate gas with the risk of exploding. I myself used smaller carbide lamps of this design while exploring caves in County Fermanagh.

Ballyhornan

Over now to the coast road to the lovely little Bay of Ballyhornan. On the Strangford side of this bay for a great many years until recently a gigantic radar dish was mounted on steel pylons. This was equivalent in height to the Belfast City Hall. The purpose of this dish was to monitor the movement of aircraft to and from the British Isles, thus maintaining a safety factor for the different air corridors. This dish was continuously revolving slowly and scanning all round. Underneath the pylons was the administration block. The area was sealed off from the general public.

'GEORGETOWN VICTORY'

Within a hundred yards of this spot out in the bay lies the sunken wreck of the 'GEORGETOWN VICTORY'. This was one of the large liberty ships returning to Britain after the end of the second world war with hundreds of sailors on board. She was bound for the Clyde

The "Georgetown Victory" at Ballyhornan Bay, 1951.

Bow section of "Georgetown Victory," 1954.

in Scotland but for some reason or other she went off course and ended up running aground here where she broke in two. It was thought that her fate here was due to compass deviation. Luckily the weather was calm and the sailors were all ferried safely ashore. When I was down the following day I saw the beach littered with hundreds of lifejackets all soaked in oil. Months later I was able to swim a short distance to the bow section and clambered aboard but because of the presence of oil still seeping from the wreck I was prevented from exploring it in any depth. This particular section was later cut up for scrap, the salvage people using acetylene burners to do this. I was glad I had taken photographs at different stages while she was still visible. Some time later she broke up and sank completely out of sight.

The origin of these liberty ships was that they were built in America in bits and pieces sometimes hundreds of miles from the sea. They were then taken to a sea port and were assembled by welding. After completion of assembly the ships were launched sideways into the water. Also if any part of a liberty ship was faulty or damaged it was replaced from another liberty ship. A lot of the parts of these liberty ships were built and assembled by women. They were sailed from America across the Atlantic to Britain where they were successfully engaged in the war effort.

Ardglass — The Herring Maidens

On a cycle run one day in 1947 to Ardglass Harbour I was excited to see the 'Herring Maidens' had arrived. These herring maidens were a group of women who journeyed around the coast of Scotland and Ireland following the shoals of herring as they moved en masse around the coast. While the fishing boats were out catching the harvest several of these women, about 24 in number, dressed in heavy protective clothing and rubber boots, were preparing the large wooden trestle tables for the cutting and gutting of the fresh herrings after being landed in Ardglass harbour.

I only once had the privilege of seeing these ladies at work. The trestle tables had corrugated iron roofs supported on pillars about five feet high above the working surface. The outside edge of the corrugated roofs overhung the table tops thus giving a little shelter during inclement weather. These trestle tables were a permanent fixture on the pier. As I stayed to watch the women at work I noticed they all had bandages around their fingers for protection. The small finger of each hand however was free of bandaging. Hose pipes swept the 'offal' into drain collectors.

A squad of men were busy withdrawing barrels of salt from the doorways leading into the hollow interior of the harbour structure. Empty barrels were stacked in rows close at hand for the ladies to pack the freshly gutted and salted fish into. When a barrel became full a wooden lid was fitted in place by the men and the barrel removed to a stacking area. From here they were then loaded into small trucks and transferred to a large steam ship berthed at the extreme end of the harbour in deep water. Onlookers like myself were discouraged from closer observation of the ship. The women whom I assumed to be Scottish sang softly in Gaelic as they worked away. One of them who appeared to be a supervisor kept parading around the tables taking charge of the whole procedure. I was delighted to have witnessed this scene but regretted not having a camera with me on that particular day. When I told my father about seeing the herring maidens he commented on how lucky I had been as he had never witnessed this scene in his lifetime.

Jordans Castle

On a day in 1948 I cycled down with my three mates Charlie Ludlow, John Wilson and Jim Cummings to Jordans Castle in Ardglass. The castle is on a hill overlooking the harbour. It was in a very poor state then. I knew, having been there a few times before, that the key was held in the local police station about a mile away, so we made our way there to sign it out. It was quite a large key about eight inches long and with this we let ourselves into the castle also taking our bicycles in. We left these on the stairway. We locked the door behind us. The Police Sergeant told us always to do this to prevent any unauthorised person or persons entering, as we were responsible once we had signed out the key. The surface of the ground floor was very irregular in its original rock formation. We discovered a false wall which we measured and realised there was a concealed room built into this part of the castle structure. We were quite excited about this and went up immediately to the chamber above. On the floor of this chamber was a large round hole. As I was the thinnest member of the party I was lowered vertically down through the hole with the lads holding my feet. As I hung there in space I shone my bicycle lamp around and reported my findings to my mates above. There was not much to report. The floor was six feet below my head and a huge domed cluster of dried up objects was all I could see. So much for the secret room. The lads started pulling me up again. This proved to be quite difficult as the hole was only about the width of my body and with me being in the upside down position my clothes bunched up as I was being drawn up again through the hole. I did have the presence of mind to keep my arms outstretched beyond my head just in case the lads would let me fall. I was finally brought up again to safety a bit bruised but none the worse for my ordeal.

I read in a book years later that the hole in the floor of castles was a primitive form of toilet. What a pity I had not read this earlier!

We continued exploring around this first chamber but all that was here was a large metal bound trunk and a few chairs. We opened the trunk but it was empty. We then went up to the chamber above. All we found here of interest was a large lump of bog butter sitting on top of a wooden box. The wooden box had the words bog butter printed on it. Bog butter was butter covered and buried in the ground in more primitive times to preserve it. This of course was before the invention of refrigerators. Occasionally samples of this butter are still being dug up on old farmsteads.

We made our way up to the top section of the castle. Outside we examined the dove cote which was in very poor condition. It had the skeletal remains of dead birds scattered around. We had a good view from here of the countryside below. As was our practice in these old buildings, we started to give the interior a bit of a clean up. We noticed a thick rope hanging down from the centre of the circular stone stairway. This was in very poor condition and was beginning to disintegrate. The original purpose of this rope was to act as a support to hold onto while going up or down the stairway but because of its dilapidated state we refrained from using it. As we had nothing therefore to hold on to, we leaned against the opposite wall while using the stairway. We locked up the castle and returned the key to the police station, signing it in again. We then proceeded on our long cycle journey home to Belfast.

Underwater Diving

Ardglass was the scene of some of my underwater adventures. In those early days my friend Billy Rodgers, his son Ronnie and I found it difficult getting our air bottles filled to the correct pressure for diving. Quite often when we went to the company for the refilled bottles they were never ready. We found this quite frustrating as it prevented us from diving. I decided to be independent and made myself a floating air pump which supplied air continuously when down to a depth of fifty feet. The air pump was positioned on a wooden platform which was hooked into the centre of an inflated tractor tube by three brackets. I used the air pump to inflate the rubber tube each time when required. The air pump or compressor had a tall plastic tube erected high above it. The compressor when switched on pumped fresh air down the plastic tube which was then relayed by air line into the air bottle on my back. On the engine side much lower down the engine exhaust gas was dispersed safely at a lower level. It was imperative that this dangerous exhaust gas was not allowed to contaminate the air feeding line. The air from the compressor to the air bottle passed through a steel bottle containing silica gel which removed any moisture present.

While using this compressor my air bottle had a modified demand valve which regulated a constant supply of air at the right pressure to a depth of approximately 50 to 60 feet under water. As long as the engine was running it was possible to stay indefinitely under water.

I found out that if I held in my left hand the rubber air feed hose from the compressor to the air cylinder on my back, I was able to feel the air pulsating through the hose so as a safety measure I kept hold of this all the time. If the air did stop pumping through I would be aware of this right away and this would have been the cue for me to surface immediately. The air in my cylinder would have allowed me about three minutes grace to do this. Although I never had to surface in an emergency when using the compressor, I did have a trial run which proved to be successful. This involved coming to the surface making sure I did not hold my breath but kept exhaling continuously all the time to prevent my lungs from being damaged by the different air pressure. By using this air compressor Billy, Ronnie and I always had an ample supply for the air bottle. We would take it in turns to explore underwater with it. I always had a red flag hoisted on the floating platform when in use. This was to alert approaching craft not to venture near it. One day whilst exploring the sea bottom in deep water off Ardglass I found a large brass cymbal which I brought ashore with me. One of the local fishermen on seeing it quipped it must have belonged to the band in Davy Jones' locker! As aqua-diving then was just beginning to gain popularity there was always a lot of interest shown by the locals in our gear and equipment. In my early days of underwater diving I actually used twin air bottles which had originated from the large experimental air line the 'BRABAZON' made by the Bristol aeroplane company. This was the prototype of the largest passenger aircraft in the world at that time. After the 'BRABAZON' had successfully completed its trials the prototype was dismantled and the parts sold. I saw the advertisement for the air bottles in a magazine and immediately purchased two of them through the post. By making a special harness I was able to adapt them into twin bottles. I still have these two cylinders to this day. Within a short distance from Ardglass was the district known as Coney Island which was comprised of an area of four to six houses. I often wondered how it got this name.

Killough

On now to Killough with its little harbour. This harbour was destroyed a great many years ago by heavy seas and was never repaired. The sea bed about half a mile out from the harbour was a favourite spot for the sub-aqua club of which I was then a member. We went to observe vast colonies of sea urchins which lived on the sea bottom here among the sand and shingle. It was a spectacular sight.

St. John's Chapel

One particular day after we had completed our diving session and changed out of our gear, I took the party about two miles away along a small country road to visit the ruins of St. John's Point Chapel. This chapel is reputed to go back as far as the seventh century. It was a very tiny chapel with the doorway only about five feet high topped by a stone lintel. All that remained was three of its walls. About a hundred yards past the ruins of the little chapel was a gateway leading to St John's Point Lighthouse. To have proceeded through the gate in order to visit the lighthouse would have required permission from the Commissioner of Irish Lights. We had to content ourselves with just observing the lighthouse from the gate but even from this distance it was quite an impressive sight.

On one occasion in 1951 I cycled past Killough through Minerstown and Tyrella to Ballykinler to visit the grave of Elsie Sands which is in a little churchyard there. There was a little plaque on the grave which read 'FRIEND OF SOLDIERS'.

Dundrum

From the graveyard I cycled to Dundrum with its castle and harbour. It was a wintry day and I took shelter in the tower bringing my bicycle inside. The entire centre of this castle from ground floor to the top was completely devoid of any structure and was only comprised of a double skin wall all round. The walls were about five feet apart and incorporated a circular stairway which led to the top of the castle. The top section of the wall was covered in most of the way round. I picked a covered-in spot and got the primus going to make a meal of soup and tea. The heat of the primus made the area warm and cosy. While I was having my soup I happened to notice a large raven who also appeared to be taking shelter. It was near the open end of the structure. It did not seem to be frightened at all and was still there about two hours later as I was preparing to leave. I left a supply of food for it and from lower down in the tower I looked up and could see the bird was enjoying its meal.

The 'DOWNSHIRE'

A few minutes from Dundrum Castle brought me down to the little harbour where I admired the steamer the 'DOWNSHIRE' which was sitting almost high and dry in the tidal harbour. One of the crew members was standing guard at the stern of the vessel and

Propellor of S.S. "Downshire," 1951.

was in communication with the engineer by means of striking a hammer on the side of the hull. Every now and again the propeller which was out of the water, would turn a few times as the engineer was working the controls inside the engine-room. I was told by the crew member that there was a slight knocking in the driveshaft on the voyage from England to Dundrum and they were trying to locate this. I took a photograph of the propeller. By this time the incoming tide began to cover the propeller and the crew member's presence was no longer required.

Newcastle

On the beach at Newcastle not far from the Percy French Memorial, about 100 yards out from high tide level was a man-made fish trap of approximately twenty four feet long by ten feet wide. This was a simple but effective means of trapping fresh fish for the Annesley Estate in the early 1900s. This fish trap was comprised of large stones set very close together in the shape of a crescent. The inner section of the crescent faced towards the land and when in proper working order the curved stone wall was perhaps a few feet high. The gaps between the stones were sealed to prevent water leaking out. When the tide came in, it would cover this structure to a depth of two to three feet and fish could swim freely along inside. When the tide receded the fish were then trapped in this man-made recess. It would then have been the job of an employee from the estate to inspect the trap and remove fish of suitable size for the kitchens. Unwanted smaller fish were left to escape on the next incoming tide. The rise and fall of the tidal level ensured the 'trap' was automatically replaced by clean water.

I saw evidence of this trap as recently as 1970. Newcastle harbour had one drawback where the boating fraternity were concerned in that it became completely dry when the tide receded. This was also a handicap to the local lifeboat. The lifeboat was kept on its trailer in the boathouse inside the harbour complex. The floor of this boathouse was on a steep slope. On call-out if the tide was in, the boat on its trailer with the men on board was released and allowed to descend to the water. It accelerated at quite a speed before it hit the water. A tank-like tractor with caterpillar wheels was always available if call-out occurred when the harbour was dry or had not enough water to allow the lifeboat to float off the trailer. This tractor towed the lifeboat on its trailer again with the men on board across the sandy harbour and out through the harbour mouth. Because the tractor had to go into the water to quite a depth to allow the lifeboat to float off the trailer, its exhaust was situated on the bonnet rising up to a height of 5 to 6 feet. The tractor then returned to the inner harbour once the lifeboat was safely afloat. I have never seen the lifeboat on genuine call-out, just on a practice run.

Annesley House

On one occasion in 1950 I visited the burned remains of the Annesley house. It was still quite an impressive ruin then. I had presumed it had been used by Army Troops at some stage and on examination of discarded bits of equipment and papers lying around I came to the conclusion that the troops had been American. In fact I discovered the burnt remains of an Army Jeep half buried near the big house. I had previously visited the estate a few times before and knew of the old dungeons and cellars underneath, which were some yards away from the house itself. One particular wet day I decided to take shelter in the dungeons which were reasonably clean.

These were situated to the north end of the main building and were about twelve feet below ground level with an approach down a gradual slope under a low roof. Two separate dungeons were side by side but separated by a thick stone wall. A shallow drain ran along the bottom of the wall which was connected to the two dungeons. It was almost dark inside except for a three inch slit up near the ceiling. As the rain outside was continuous I decided to pass the time by exploring the limited confines of one of these dungeons, choosing the one furthest away from the sea. I was able to dislodge a length of heavy stone which revealed a large cavity

From left to right — Sammy, Richard, Noel and Jack in dungeons of Annesley Estate, Newcastle, 1961.

in the wall. I had my bicycle lamp with me as I squeezed my body through into this cavity which was about eight yards square. The roof was wedge shaped tapering from shoulder height to ground level. I felt fresh cold air blowing from the tapered end of the cavity. I crawled along to this part to investigate but could not find any opening so was forced to retreat. The roof of this cavity was really the thick floor of the two dungeons above and I could see the outlets of the dungeon drains which went in the direction of the sea. I had difficulty emerging out of the cavity again and, when through, was somewhat bruised and scratched but otherwise delighted to have found the hidden cavity. I carefully replaced the large block of stone. Under the centre of the house itself were deep cellars one of which was about five yards square. The open doorways had a half round stone topping. They were devoid of wood not having any doors. There was no provision for lighting at all and although there was a strong smell of dampness, the rooms were clean.

During one of my visits there with my friends Sammy Craig, Jack Lavelle and Richard Young, we emerged from these cellars up to the ground floor but not before I had set the camera with the self timer 'Ticking Annie' to take a photo of the four of us in one of the dungeons. We then entered the ruins of the conservatory which was almost devoid of glass. We were interested to see that the glass of the roof section was slightly curved giving it a pleasing domed effect which in its original state must have looked quite impressive.

Chapter 11
THE MOURNES

American Fighter Plane

One day in 1949 whilst walking in the Mournes on Chimney Rock I came across the remains of the wings and parts of the fuselage, including the propeller, of an American Fighter Aircraft. This plane, which I believed to be a CORSAIR, crashed during the Second World War years of 1939-45. It was lying upside down with the engine and cockpit missing. I was puzzled at the time by the absence of these. The wings of the plane immediately at the fuselage had a downward slope, the reason for this was to give ground clearance for the propeller when the plane was sitting on its undercarriage. From the undercarriage point outwards the wings had an upward slope. This was quite a unique design known as 'gullwing' and enabled the abnormally large propeller to be used on a low-winged aircraft. The very large propeller of this particular plane had three blades.

I was quite excited at finding this plane and I searched around in vain for the engine and cockpit. When I got home I thought continuously about it and a few weeks later I went back to Chimney Rock. I traced the flight path from the aeroplane's first contact with the mountain where it left trimming tabs and further on pieces of the tail assembly to the entire fuselage and wings etc. Finally after careful planning and searching I managed to locate the missing sections almost a quarter of a mile to the East and several hundred feet away in a gully lower down the mountain. The engine and cockpit which were joined together were in an upright position. This allowed me to actually sit in the cockpit which showed charred signs of being burnt by intense heat. Otherwise the engine etc. was in very good order. I was able to open an inspection door and saw a nameplate which I took home for a souvenir and which had the following details on it:

SOLAR ANTI-MONOXIDE EXHAUST MANIFOLD
SOLAR AIRCRAFT COMPANY SAN DIEGO

MODEL
B-26B

(TRIANGLE LOGO)

DEL DATE
3-11-42

DRAWING
NO.12-711

SERIAL NO.
1125

CONTRACT NO.
W535-AC-16137
W535-AO-13244

MATERIAL SPEC
AN-QQ-S-757

MANUFACTURED BY:
EDWARD G BUDD MANUFACTURING COMPANY
PHILADELPHIA, PENNSYLVANIA.

top — REG
L/Side — TRADE
R/Side — MARK
INSIDE TRIANGLE SYMBOL OF TRADE MARK

Wellington Bomber

The war brought a few other military aircraft casualties to the Mournes. This was probably due to the fact that the flight path from England to Aldergrove and Belfast passed over the Mourne Mountains. One of these was a Wellington Bomber which I also saw in 1950. I actually came across this by accident while taking a different walking route up to Donard peak from the direction of Tullybrannigan. I was astonished when I stumbled upon the large radial engine of this plane so far down the mountain and so close to Newcastle. The engine which was partly embedded in the earth was about five feet high above the ground. I started searching the vicinity and about eight yards away I found the second engine which was covered in brambles. Both of the engines were in very poor condition. Their respective propellers were badly twisted around the engine couplings where they had rotated right up to the point of contact with the mountain. This plane also showed signs of severe burning.

Some yards further back were the scant remains of the wings and fuselage. The latter still had several lengths of the famous Geodetic construction which gave enormous strength to the aeroplane's fuselage. The Wellington Bomber was designed by Barnes Wallace of 'Bouncing Bomb' fame. One night in 1975 my wife and I along with our friends Derek and Ann Henderson were visiting a relation in Newcastle. I surprised Derek by walking him in the darkness up to the remains of the Wellington Bomber. Parts of one of the engines had disappeared — probably taken by souvenir hunters. Derek was also quite amazed as to the close proximity of this air crash to the town.

Mosquito Fighter Bomber

On the top of Commedagh (meaning 'the mountain of watching') and on the Kilkeel side of the mountain lies the scattered remains of a Mosquito Fighter Bomber which I also saw in 1950. The top of Commedagh must have been the first point of contact and here can be seen the remains of the hydraulic fittings of the Mosquito. The plane had then slid down on the Kilkeel side of the mountain where the tail plane assembly was still intact in a gully. There was practically nothing left of the fuselage but at the bottom of the gully were two large Rolls Royce Merlin engines. Incidentally one of the engines was periodically covered by sliding shale while the other was always exposed. The latter was in less perfect condition due to bits and pieces being taken for souvenirs. The almost vertical gully

Part of wheel unit of Mosquito Bomber crashed in Mournes about 1943.

Eddie and Chris Griffiths with Rita at one of Mosquito engines in Mournes, 1974.

Noel, Chris and Eddie at wheel of Mosquito in Mournes, 1974.

Castles of Commedagh, the Mournes, 1950.

levels out gradually to a gentle sloping valley still in the direction of Kilkeel and here, a quarter of a mile from the engines, lay one of the large undercarriage wheels. The Mosquito, made by De Havilland was unusual in that it was mostly of wooden construction making it much lighter for speed. Because of this it was one of the most successful British military aircraft. It had a top speed of 400 mph being powered by two Merlin Rolls Royce engines. The planes were fitted with four cannons which gave great fire power. To enable the planes to go faster the cannons were sheeted over with plastic paper which would be blown away when the guns would fire. The Germans used the dreaded 'DOODLEBUG' flying bombs over England which went on a set course and could not be changed. The distance was too great for them to reach Northern Ireland. In England these could be heard flying overhead. When the engines stopped this was when they fell and exploded so it was a warning for people below to immediately take cover. However one of the Mosquito pilots found he could fly alongside and by using the tip of his plane wing he could overturn the 'DOODLEBUG' while over barren country making it fall to the ground to explode harmlessly away from built up areas.The pilot found this also saved his ammunition.

Unidentified Aircraft Wreckage

Not far from the Castles of Commedagh which are rocky projections on top of the mountain, can also be found parts of an aircraft engine. There was not enough wreckage left to identify the type of aircraft these belonged to but I estimated it to be a much older plane than the Mosquito. I visited this wreckage again in 1961 with my three friends Richard Young, Sammy Craig and Jack Lavelle.

From left: Richard Young, Noel, Jack Lavelle and Sammy Craig inspecting unidentified aircraft engine in Mournes, 1961.

Weather Balloon

The summer of 1950 was very poor weatherwise and on one of my visits to the Mournes, the ground was so water-logged that the prospect of wet feet after the cycle run from Belfast to Bloody Bridge in the Mourne Mountains caused me to change direction. So after leaving my bicycle in safe hands at a small cottage on the edge of the Mournes, I began to ascend one of the smaller ridges. Once

Weather balloon transmitting equipment found in Mournes, 1950.

past the water pipe line which feeds Belfast and County Down with fresh drinking water, I began the more taxing climb up the slopes of Spences Mountain which is only 1,535 feet above sea level. Nearing the summit I saw an object which was grey in colour lying among the heather. Being wary of unexploded ammunition left around from the Second World War, I had a careful look around and discovered several objects all in a straight line from North to South. I then realised it was a weather balloon instrument. The balloon itself was missing but on opening the casing I found a lovely little radio transmitter connected to various instruments. I surmised these would record temperature, humidity and other atmospheric conditions and the transmitter would relay the information back to earth as the balloon travelled on its predetermined path. As the apparatus was of considerable weight I assumed the device would descend by parachute or the gas in the balloon would be gradually reduced to allow a gentle landing. Because of the distance between the objects I also assumed the balloon had still been attached during the last minutes of flight. Electric power for transmitting the information obtained in flight back to a ground station was provided by a lovely little accumulator which was powered by a jellied substance. Transmission was from radio valves, themselves quite large and heavy. Of course this was before the advent of the tiny transistor. I still have in my possession most of the accessories of this weather balloon including the transmitter with its glass radio valves.

In later years a reward was offered for the return of these balloons with transmitting equipment. While cycling through Belfast one day I watched a group of children trying to capture one of these as it descended amongst traffic on the Antrim Road.

Quarry Machinery

While I was searching in 1950 in the valley on the other side of Chimney Rock in relation to the 'CORSAIR', I spotted machinery associated with quarrying. At that particular time I was concentrating more on the crashed CORSAIR but I made a mental note to return at a later date to study the quarry machinery. So the following year I decided to spend a weekend at that spot. After returning home from work one Friday evening from the Shipyard, I had my dinner and prepared to set off for the Mournes on my bicycle. Because my bivouac tent was quite heavy I decided to take a lighter makeshift one, together with foodstuffs and other equipment.

It was a beautiful evening and I enjoyed the long cycle run down to the Mournes. Close to Ballagh Bridge I left my bicycle at a cottage and also left with the lady a diagram depicting the area where I would be encamped. After leaving Ballagh Bridge I climbed the slopes of Spence's Mountain. It was easy going along the wide valley through which the River Spence flowed. I was surrounded here by Mullartown Upper, Rocky Mountain, Chimney Rock and Spence's Mountain. I found a site there which consisted of four walls about five feet high and twelve square which had probably been an enclosure for sheep at some time. The walls were constructed of stone dyking and it was within these four walls that I pitched my tent.

As darkness approached I sat looking out over the sea at the far off island of Lambey off the Dublin coast almost sixty miles to the South. The sky was clear with a partial full moon and once my eyes became accustomed to the surrounding area I found the local visibility good enough to entice me to leave my tent to explore further up the valley. Here I came across a four-wheeled truck which was lying on its side half buried in soil. As time was not important to me I sat down and pondered on the valley's secrets. High above I heard birds calling to each other as they flew in the moonlight towards the North East.

I returned to my tent and turned in for the night. The next morning I was up very early and made my breakfast on the small methylated burner which I brought with me because it was much lighter than the primus stove. My eyes began to water a little with the fumes. After breakfast I packed my haversack and, leaving the tent, I proceeded to walk along the valley. As I made my way along the tracks in the ground I came to the quarry area where the valley got broader and deeper. This was brought about by removal of vast quantities of sand. It was as if time had stood still here for at various places among little hillocks were several four wheeled steel buggies on which were 'V' shaped containers. These were pivoted along the bottom of the 'V' to enable them to be tipped over on either side as required to empty the contents. These buggies were operated on tracks smaller but similar to those used by narrow gauge railways. One of these buggies was at the bottom of a shallow incline. I pushed it up the incline and got into it and enjoyed the short run to the bottom. I found that only two of the buggies could be pushed along, the others were solid with rust. A lot of the track line was missing. Among other items of interest were seven steel, almost heart shaped concave shovels with long wooden handles about nine feet long. When I attempted to lift a shovel full of soil I found it was almost beyond my strength to do so. The quarry men who had used these must have been very strong indeed.

On the left hand side of Spence's River in among boulders were little tool box containers, all in the last stage of decay. I spent long hours all that day just strolling around the area. I have visited a few old quarries in my day but none of them had so much expensive equipment left to deteriorate and rust away and I wondered what would have brought this about.

From the condition of the various trolleys and other equipment, it was obvious they had not been used for the best part of half a century perhaps going back to the 1920s. I returned to my tent settling down for another night. The next morning whilst having breakfast I was aware of the weather beginning to change. I broke camp, packing all my gear, and took a different route back towards O'Rourke's Park and followed the water pipeline back towards

Ballagh Bridge. By this time there was a distinct dampness in the air. I called at the cottage to collect my bicycle and had quite a long chat with the lady there. She was very interested to know what was over the mountain as she had never been there herself. I packed my gear onto my bicycle and after bidding the lady farewell I began the thirty mile cycle run home. I had found it most remarkable to be able to walk for miles with such beautiful scenery without meeting another person. I spent many happy hours over the years at different times wandering over the Mournes, always on the lookout for anything of interest. On one of my early visits in 1947 on the slopes of CLONACHULLION (meaning 'meadow, swampy or river bank') just at SPELLACK ridge, I stumbled on the remains of a main lifting beam of a small wooden crane which had been used by the granite stone cutters to lift blocks of granite rocks perhaps as far back as the 1920s. The whole crane was buried horizontally in wet moss. The beam alone was about 20 feet long and on it I could see a name plate partially exposed. I dug with my bare hands removing moss and undergrowth until I finally uncovered the whole name plate which was screwed onto the main lifting beam of the crane. The name plate was in the shape of a shield and turned out to be quite elaborate. After quite a while working with stones as tools I managed to prise it off minus a corner which is still attached to the crane on the mountain. I brought the name plate home. It was made of cast iron. Embossed at the top was a green thistle with purple flower. Below this the name JOHN GRAY and on the next line UDDINGSTON, and on the next line BY GLASGOW. These last three lines are painted in brown. On the next line 1 TON is painted in yellow while the next line has the word PATENT and the last line the words DERRICK CRANE. These last two lines are painted in brown. All the words like the emblem of the thistle are embossed. The shield is quite artistic in relation to modern day standards.

Heavy Snowfall 1949

In February 1949 heavy snow had fallen over Northern Ireland and the County Down area was covered to a depth of several inches. Charlie Ludlow, John Wilson and I, after having driven around in the snow in our motorised bikes, decided to take on a challenge against the elements. The following day was Sunday and we all set off early for the Mournes. Charlie and John were both on a Phillips 50 cc bike with the registration Nos. TZ-874 and TZ-876 and I was on a 25 cc Cyclemaster powered bicycle OZ-1204.

We made reasonable time from Belfast to Newcastle. The Phillips machines were vastly superior in power and performance to my lowly Cyclemaster. Being early on the road the snow was soft and quite safe to ride over. We branched across country via Tollymore Park, (Tollymore meaning 'the big hill') where we stopped to thaw out our frozen legs and enjoy a hot meal prepared on my primus stove. We then set off on the steep climb past the Fofanny Dam reservoir, near the source of the river Shimna (meaning 'river of the reeds or rushes'). This was on the Slieve Meelmore side of the road up the incline to meet the road from Hilltown near the Spelga River at the Deers Meadow. It is here that in latter years the huge Spelga Dam was built when a great catchment area was flooded for this purpose. Also for the record the source of the River Bann is at the Deers Meadow.

Up the Mournes in snow on the two Phillips machines and Cyclemaster, Feb. 1949.

Closer view of Phillips TZ-874 which I purchased later from my friend, 1958.

At the Deers Meadow the snow drifts were between two and three feet deep and although the two Phillips machines were capable of driving through it with assistance by pedalling, it was beyond the capability of the lower powered Cyclemaster to do so and at this point we decided to call it a day. We first chose a snow bank to shelter behind while we started up the primus on which we heated soup which was greatly appreciated by the three of us. It was while relaxing with the hot soup that a quiet word from Charlie drew our attention and we literally froze in our movements for walking past was a beautiful badger and he had not spotted us in the snow bunker. He continued across the snow in the direction of Slieve Muck and disappeared from view. Unfortunately I had no film left in the camera to photograph 'Brock' as he passed us in the snow.

It was time to go as dusk was setting in fast and the roads would be more dangerous with other traffic churning the snow into mush. The return journey was safe enough and we stopped at Ballynahinch to make hot tea before proceeding on home.

One morning in the summer of 1949 I cycled again down to Newcastle and after leaving my bike in safe keeping I started walking up the familiar track through the trees to the stile that separated the woodland from the bare mountain. It was not really bare because heather grew all the way up. I stopped for a bite to eat at one of my popular spots, the Ice House. While sitting admiring the wonderful scenery three hikers were passing and stopped for a chat. It was only when talking to them that I realised two of the men were blind. They both wore loose belts around their waists and they explained that these were used to connect to each other when ascending the steep slopes. Their guide told me they were bound for the summit of Donard where they would rest before returning down again. I noted the guide had a camera with him to record the feat. I had the greatest admiration for the two blind hikers whose enthusiasm would have put any sighted person to shame.

Stream Blockage

Once while leaving my bicycle at a farmhouse near the Trassey River, the farmer asked my help to trace a blockage in his stream further up the mountain from which he used the water for his turbine-driven electric generator. He mentioned some boys had altered the flow further up and this prevented him using the generator to milk his cows. He said this problem happened quite often. I promised him I would trace the offending blockage. Sure enough as I made my way up the higher slopes of CLONACHULLION I came across boulders right across the stream diverting the water in another direction. I hastily re-routed the water supply to its original course by removing the boulders and I followed the stream to even higher slopes to ensure there were no other blockages. While on this route I also discovered two primitive shelters isolated from each other. These would have been used by individual granite stone cutters. The shelters were now disused and in very poor condition.

Having spent most of that day in the mountains, I headed down again. On reaching the farmhouse to collect my bicycle, I was happy to hear the generator going and see the farmhouse lit up. I found a large strong reinforced paper bag of fresh eggs tied to the handlebar of my bicycle. The farmer came out to thank me personally and after thanking him for the eggs and saying my farewell, I headed for home which was a four hour cycle run. I managed to get the eggs home intact much to my parents' delight.

The Little Fish on the Mountain

On another day in 1961 when I was walking from the site of the old derrick crane I cut across the valley to Luke's Mountain. As I was ascending the slopes here at about the 800 feet level, I happened to be stepping over some very wet heather when a movement caught my eye. It was a little fish about seven inches long, similar in looks but a lot longer than the more common stickleback or smick. It wriggled bit by bit ever upward in the wet heather. It would rest awhile, rubbing its head in the wet grass and then continued on for another short distance. When it stopped each time I could see its little gills going in and out. I could only guess at that time that its purpose was to climb higher to spawn. At one stage I actually cupped it in my hands to help it over an obstacle and set it down gently again, watching it persevere on its journey. I was really captivated by its determination. I found out later there was a small lake on a plateau further up which must have been its destination.

On another day while setting off for the Mournes, I decided to explore further up the left hand side of Luke's Mountain. Before I approached the gate at Hare's Gap I came across a little shelter made of four stone dyke walls with a corrugated roof. The shelter stood about four feet high. Although the walls were still intact the corrugated roof was almost corroded away by rust. I crawled inside and was amazed to discover a small manually operated fan blower.

This would have been used by the granite stone cutters to temper or harden their chisels. Constant chipping into the hard granite would have made the chisel quite blunt from time to time and these would be sharpened by placing them, after filing, on a small camp like fire and turning the handle of the fan blower to direct a fast current of air to flow through a small aperture. This in turn made the fire white hot. The granite cutter would then determine the correct moment to quench the chisels in cold water. He would then have re-heated them again to a lesser degree of heat, re-dipping them again in cold water. This second operation would have tempered them making them hard but non-brittle. I was surprised to find this fan blower in quite good condition. I tried the handle myself and a blast of air came out of the nozzle signifying it was still in good working order. I knew of at least four of these shelters at different locations on the Mournes which would have been used by the granite stone cutters but the other three were completely empty except for a few badly corroded chisels and files. This particular shelter with the fan blower was probably the last one to be used. Also in the shelter was an iron casting which was rectangular in shape with serrated slats all slanting upwards. This device was used to hold a block of granite in the slats at an angle, keeping it in place while the workmen would chip away at the granite surface. I have seen several of these castings scattered about the Mournes. I also found in this shelter a mug which had been cleverly fashioned out of a syrup tin with a neatly made wooden handle. I was so impressed with the ingenuity shown in the making of this that I brought it home to show to my parents.

The Hare in the Cave

Quite a few times while I was walking in the Mournes I would have been caught in heavy showers. A favourite spot for me to take shelter on these occasions was under an overhanging large rock in the area known as SPELLACK. This overhanging rock formed a cave like structure underneath. It was always dry and comfortable. When I looked out from here straight across I could see the quarry men working at the last surviving quarry site while above them at a higher level I could see the Hare's Gap.

On one occasion while sheltering in this particular crevice, I was having my lunch with a flask of tea. I happened to notice over to my left a large hare sitting in an upright position with its front paws outstretched. It seemed to be watching me intently. Perhaps like me it was also taking shelter from the heavy rain outside. It did not seem in the least frightened and I was quite taken with its presence. In fact while I was having my lunch it seemed to become quite relaxed and I was infatuated when it started to wash itself by licking its paw and then bringing it round to the back of one of its large ears rubbing vigorously. It then repeated this action with the other ear. I threw some food over towards the hare but it did not seem interested. When I had finished my lunch I decided to lie down and have a rest as it was still raining quite heavily. Imagine my surprise when the hare also decided to lie down. It was lying down with its paws outstretched on the ground and its head over on one side still watching me. After about an hour the rain started to ease off and I decided to head back. I collected together all my equipment and leaving some food for my furry companion, I left the cave like shelter. The hare still remained there. I felt quite privileged at seeing a hare at such close quarters. Indeed I found it quite a comical experience.

I decided to go back a different way by rounding the lower slopes of the north side of Slieve Meelmore, making my way back by Clonachullion, crossing over the Trassey River and back to my bicycle.

'Ticking Annie'

Another day while up in the Mournes I decided to go to the top of Slieve Bearnagh which is at a height of 2,394 feet. It was a glorious day and I spent most of the time there. This particular day in 1953 I had my camera with me together with self timer. This timer was of ex-British Army War Department stock which I purchased in a surplus ex-army store in Belfast. It was actually a self timer for a delayed action bomb. It had jewel movements in it and when modifying it for photography purposes I removed these. Its maximum delayed time duration was approximately seventy five minutes. When it was set the ticking noise was quite loud and could be heard a few yards away and my pet name for it was 'Ticking Annie'. I tried an experiment with it on the top of Slieve Bearnagh with the camera pointing down towards the Silent Valley. I set the timer to maximum then raced as fast as I could down to a lower plateau which I had previously focused in on with the viewfinder. I placed myself in a predetermined position and there I had to wait for over an hour to ensure that the photograph had been taken. I was about a quarter of a mile away from the camera so was completely out of hearing distance of the ticking sound. I had then to walk the same distance back to retrieve the camera.

I was very pleased a few days later when I developed the film which included the back view of me standing looking down over the Silent Valley.

Noel looking out over Silent Valley, 1953.

Noel at what looked like a giant's head, scratching its nose — taken at Slieve Bearnagh with "Ticking Annie," 1960.

Quarry Men at Work

On my way down from Slieve Bearnagh the same day I came down through the Hare's Gap and through the gate. 200 yards from here I turned into the quarry on my left. This was the working I had previously looked over at from SPELLACK. There were about five men working there. They invited me into their hut to share a can of tea. The home made buns my mother had baked were much appreciated by them. The men were rugged and weather beaten. Their hands were roughened with years of working in the elements with the hard granite. Although I found them to be a bit reserved at first, they were nevertheless sincere and homely. I enjoyed the opportunity of conversing with them. They spoke of the times when granite was in great demand. When they heard I worked in the Shipyard they showed a great deal of interest not only in that but in the outside world in general. We sat in the hut which had no windows and talked around an open fire.

Because the stovepipe chimney was too small a lot of smoke drifted out through the open door. However the pungent smoke and fumes finally drove me outside with my eyes streaming. The men had a hearty laugh at this. They all came out to continue their work and allowed me the privilege of staying to watch them. I was able to observe that they did not use explosives for blasting out the rock. Instead they drilled two holes of about one inch diameter.

The holes were about a yard apart. They did this with a manual drill. Into the two holes they then inserted long tapered steel wedges. Two of the men then started tapping lightly in unison with hammers at the respective wedges. Suddenly the granite split right down the seam resulting in a section of granite being separated. The other men then wedged this out of position, laying it aside. It was then examined by what seemed to be the foreman who told me he was looking for hair-line cracks. Once he gave it the 'all clear' it was then laid aside with other sections to await collection. I was lucky enough to witness a huge solid block of choice granite about 8-ft by 4-ft by 4-ft being hewn out. The men told me this was a special order and was to be used as a centre-piece for a new building in Belfast.

On the site was an old ex-army open lorry in very poor condition. This was used to relay the smaller sections down to the main road for further collection, while the heavier sections were transported right from the quarry site in specialised modern lorries to their destination. I saw this old military lorry at a later date lying abandoned further down the mountain side. It was obviously past its usefulness.

The Diamond Rocks

Another time up the Mournes I headed for the Hare's Gap which I always considered to be the gateway to the Mournes. My mission this time was to search for the area known as the Diamond Rocks. I climbed over the gate at the Hare's Gap and onto the Brandy Pad or Path. The Brandy Path got its name from times long gone when it was alleged that Smugglers used this route to transport brandy and spirits away from the vigilance of Customs Officers. Erosion has taken its toll along this most famous stretch of the Mournes

David Beattie walking along the Brandy Path in the summer of 1976.

David Beattie in the snow at the Mourne Wall, in the Hare's Gap, early 1960s.

and even as far back as the 1950s long lengths of the path were being reduced to bare white stone as can be seen in the photograph.

Erosion has also worn away the surface at the bends making walking very difficult and I wondered even then how long this beautiful part of the Mournes would be enjoyed by hikers and hill walkers alike. In fact this is why the famous 'Mourne Wall Walk' was stopped in recent years. 1983 was the last year it was held.

Less than a quarter of a mile along the Brandy Path on the left hand side I ascended a very steep slope and came to an eroded section where I found in abundance sections of rocky quartz. By examining these more closely I was able to pick out lumps of multi-faceted quartz. It is probably because of the presence of these quartz that this particular area became known as the Diamond Rocks.

The Swarm of Bees

I climbed up further from the Diamond Rocks to the ridge of Slievenaglogh (meaning 'the mountain of stones') and was staying close to the east side of the Mourne Wall for protection from the strong south wind. At Slieve Corragh which was at a height of 2,250 feet a strange thing happened. I saw swarms of bees rising and falling in the strong wind. As I approached close to them I could see their problem was not the wind alone but the fact that a violent vacuum-like down draft caused by a rush of air over the Mourne Wall which was about six feet high by four feet wide, was preventing them from proceeding over the mountain to the other side. I was quite close to the bees yet felt no fear of them. I let a swarm of them walk unto a sheet of paper I was holding and then gently inserted it through a gap in the wall. The bees then managed to take off safely on the other side. I repeated this several times. The bees then started going through the gap themselves. They were very much smaller than the ones found in the garden at home. I was fascinated as I watched them crawl through the gap and when they were a short distance beyond the wind barrier, they took off still flying close to the ground until they successfully flew off down the hillside in the direction of Kilkeel. If I had not been there to see for myself I would not have believed the bees actually flew in swarms over the Mourne mountains. If they had gained a higher altitude before arriving at the Mourne Wall I do not think they would have encountered the problem of the down draft.

The Ice House

One day in the early 1950s it was planned that I, along with my friends Charlie Ludlow, John Wilson and Jim Cummings, would climb to the top of Donard, staying overnight in order to see the sunrise over the Irish Sea which we were told was quite a spectacular sight.

I drove the boys down on the Friday night in my Ford Anglia. The weather was good and we had a pleasant drive down. I parked the car at Tullybrannigan and with our packs we ascended the lower slopes of the Donard. We decided while there we would first explore the Ice House before going further. Before the advent of refrigerators, large estates had their own ice houses which were usually situated quite a distance from the big houses they served. These ice houses were packed solid with blocks of ice and small quantities were removed as and when required. The ice would have been taken from the rivers during the winter months when it became available and stored in the ice houses for later use. I remember my father telling me that in his day during some of the mild winters when there was no local ice available, it was brought by ship from Norway to Newcastle Harbour.

Several ice houses can still be found around the country. One very good example can be still seen to this day at Belvoir Park, Belfast. We reached this particular ice house in the Mournes by climbing up the Donard path. We assumed this chiefly served the Annesley Estate in Newcastle. It was situated on the left at the edge of the Glen river. This ice house was in reasonable order. It was built of brick and was circular in shape with a domed roof in the centre of which was a round ventilator hole. The entrance was through two metal doors, one on the outside and the other inside. The purpose of the two doors was to allow the first door to be closed before opening the second thus ensuring a minimum change in temperature when the ice house was in operation. As we entered the first door we made sure it was left open for safety. We had to take care when opening the second door that we did not fall into the ice chamber as the walls were sheer all round. On the left hand side were recessed hand and foot holds down to the bottom. We had to use our lamps as it was quite dark. We started to climb down the vertical descent which was about 10 feet. It was a hair-raising experience hanging on by our finger tips at times. We finally reached the bottom and when we looked up we could see the stars shining down through the little ventilator hole in the centre of the roof. We found inside was cosy enough to have a cup of tea which we made on the primus stove. On the bottom of the ice chamber we discovered in the very centre of the floor a small drain which would have, in its day, drained off any melted ice.

After we had our tea we then made our way up out of the ice chamber and resumed our climb up the Donard to the summit. We arrived at the stone room which was really the corner post of the boundary wall going round the Mournes. Although it only consisted of one chamber it was quite ornate looking on the outside and was rectangular in shape with a pillar like top. The boundary wall enclosed the property belonging to the Water Commissioners.

We entered the doorway opening into the little stone room. On

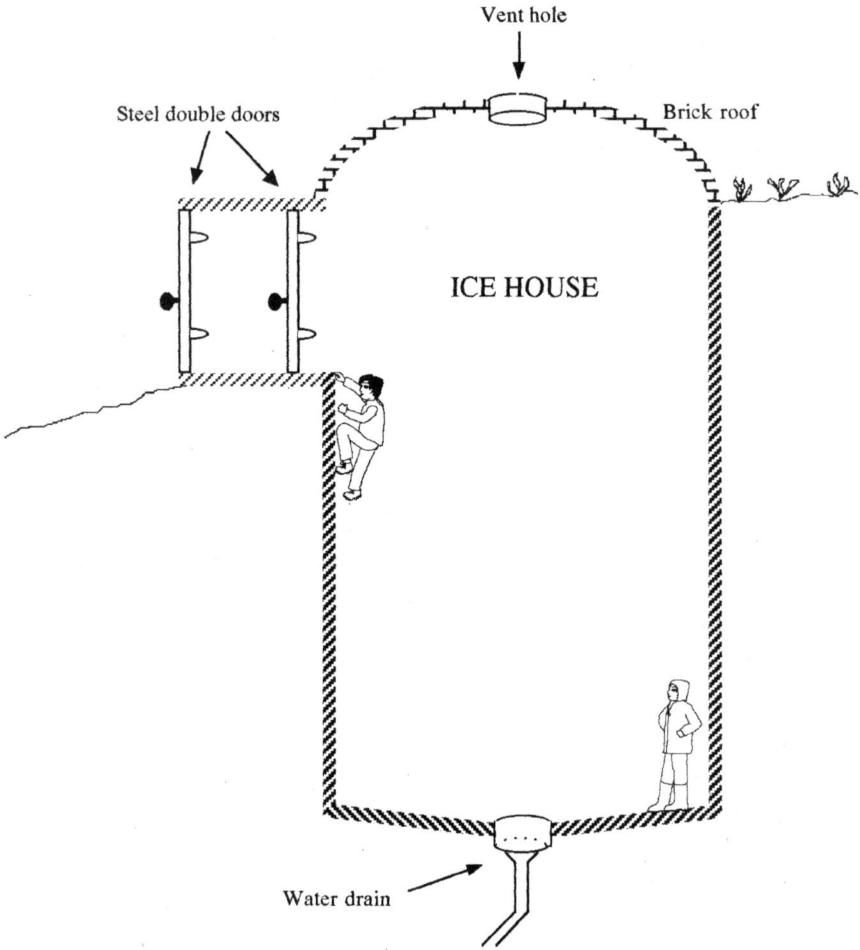

Sketch of Ice House in the Mournes as it was in the 1950s.

the left hand side the floor was raised approximately two feet which formed a seat. The four of us, now quite tired, settled down to sleep or so we thought. The strong North wind rushed past the opening causing a vacuum which hurt our ears. We all pulled our blankets over our heads and must have fallen asleep. We woke up to a glorious dawn casting its light over the Mournes but we were quite annoyed with ourselves at missing the sunrise as the weather had been just perfect for it. We must have slept right through it. We gathered all our belongings and forced our aching limbs to trudge down the steep slopes. We again stopped at the Ice House to have a quick brew up on the primus stove before making our way back to the car and home. There was no talk of our adventures on the way back as my three friends had fallen fast asleep. I had to keep the window of the car down to keep myself awake. To this day I still have not had the pleasure of seeing the Sunrise over the Mournes.

The Cashel Sleeper

Another morning about the same period I left on my push bike for a planned trip from Belfast to Kilkeel. The morning was dry and warm and with the wind on my back I made quite good speed. On arriving at Clough I decided on the spur of the moment to change course and headed instead for Lough Island Reavey. At the beginning of the lake there was a road which passed the wooded hillside of Moneyscalp and came out at Tollymore Forest Park. My objective was only a short distance along the road to the well known Cashel souterrain (underground chamber). This consisted of a long passage underground with steps at each end leading to the surface while off the passageway underneath and to one side, was a room of about 16 feet long by six and a half feet wide with seven feet headroom. This souterrain was only a few hundred yards from the road.

The passageway and the room were completely dark. As I made my way with the aid of my bicycle lamp down the passageway and into the room I shone my lamp around the roof and almost fell over an old man sleeping on bundles of straw. This gave me quite a fright as I did not expect to meet anyone here. I must have frightened the man who turned out to be a harmless tramp. However, I soon put him at his ease. He told me he used the soutterain often on his journey from Newry to Ballynahinch as well as other little sheltered hides along the road. I found this man to be a mine of local knowledge and his eyes really lit up when I produced a flask of tea and shared my food with him. At no time did he ask for money and when I left to continue my journey I gave the 'Cashel Sleeper' half of my day's supply of food. I had almost forgotten about my meeting with him until a few years later, early one morning after camping near the White Water mountain stream between Rostrevor and Kilkeel. I was returning home to Belfast by the mountain road from Kilkeel to Dundrum on my twin cylinder L.E. Velocette motor cycle. As I approached the Deer's Meadow, a solitary man was walking in the same direction. I stopped and offered him a lift which he gratefully accepted. My passenger was really taken with the uncanny silence of the machine. He was good crack and the miles sped by as I listened to his stories of the mountain roads. His destination was Ballynahinch where he had prospects of occasional work on local farms there. As it was on my route I was able to leave him off at the entrance to an estate and it was only as we parted I realised he was going for a job to the same estate as the 'Cashel sleeper' I had previously met a few years before in the souterrain. I always found it quite interesting to meet these men of the road and share a little time in their company.

Silent Valley Overflow

While visiting the beautiful setting of the Silent Valley reservoir I often admired the large funnel shaped structure surrounded by water at the Scardan Hill end of the reservoir. This stonework structure measured approximately fifteen feet in diameter. It was an artistically designed overflow which had a vertical drop down into the ground. When the water rose above the rim of this structure it flowed over into the funnel down the large tapered hole in the centre which led down to a large pipe. This excess water was discharged into the Kilkeel river and eventually dispersed into the sea at Kilkeel Bay. The structure maintained an even balance of water and ensured the dam walls were not threatened or damaged by pressure and weight of excess water. Of the many times I was there I never ever witnessed the overflow being actually put to the test. An underground tunnel was blasted right through Slieve Binnian which drained water into the Silent Valley reservoir from a large catchment area on the other side of this mountain. In the 1950s I knew the blasting had been completed on this tunnel but final finishing had not taken place. My friend Eddie Hunter and I decided early one morning to cycle from Belfast. We arrived at Newcastle, on to Annalong and up to Rourke's Park. There we left our bicycles for safe custody and started to walk in the direction of the newly hewn out tunnel. Our feet were quite wet walking over sodden ground as we arrived at the impressive tunnel entrance.

I had estimated this to be about one mile long so brought enough lighting equipment to take us through the tunnel, not forgetting the return journey. I hoped the tunnel would bring us out into the Silent Valley near the overflow pipe. For me it was a bit like potholing but for Eddie it was quite a new experience. We began in the tunnel with a headroom of 10 feet and although this diminished a bit we were able to continue walking upright all the way. We quickly lost all traces of daylight and then relied on our carbide gas lamps which gave off a good amount of heat as well as light. We made reasonable progress until the floor became very rough and we found ourselves stepping into deep puddles of ice cold water. Although our feet were wet and numb with the cold we were glad we had worn shorts for cycling as it would have been more unpleasant with wet trouser legs as well.

Eventually daylight shone in front of us and we approached the end of the tunnel. However we were in for a disappointment. We could not get out because there was a deep gully the width of the tunnel which was full of water. As we did not wish to swim in the ice cold water, we had no option but to trudge all the way back to our starting point. It had taken us three hours to walk to the end of the tunnel and back. It was quite an unforgettable experience for we both realised we would never have the chance again to walk under Binnian once the flow of water was directed along it.

We stood again in bright sunlight, completely frozen with soaking wet feet. We were thankful for the heat from the rays of the sun as we set off again and still managed to enjoy our 40 mile cycle run home with a treasured memory for the future.

Ben Crom Reservoir

The Ben Crom reservoir which is situated a short distance to the right and above the Silent Valley was built much later. One week before it was officially closed off and the water allowed to build up in the huge dam, I decided to walk the full length of the new reservoir. Thousands of others decided to do the same. We walked the full length of a mile and a quarter almost right up to the dam wall. It was quite an historic occasion as we all knew we would never

Ben Crom Reservoir, 1962.

again in our lifetime walk along the valley floor.

One early morning in 1962 I took a trip on my L.E. Velocette motor cycle from Belfast down to Bloody Bridge which is a few miles beyond Newcastle, Co. Down. After leaving the machine in safe keeping with local people I climbed over the wall which separated the main road from a very steep gorge down to the sea in the vicinity of the little inlet known locally as 'Williams Harbour'. This inlet is between Ballagh Bridge and Bloody Bridge. From here I began to walk along the rocky coastline in the direction of Annalong. This terrain was quite rugged and rough but at the same time very pleasant. At times I was confronted with barbed wire which forced me to walk on the seaward side to ensure I was not trespassing.

On this particular morning the wind was from the west and I was protected by high banks. It made the sea walk feel as if I was in a vacuum which to say the least felt very strange, causing me to swallow frequently for ear balance. As I had all day to enjoy this walk I spent time exploring the flotsam among the rocks. I found a dark green glass ball of five inches diameter. In those days these were used by fishermen as floats for their nets. The floats of today are made of plastic. I was delighted with my find and even more so when I came across another one of the same size but this one was clear glass. I found the second one jammed between rocks by the rough seas. In fact it took quite a lot of force to dislodge it.

I continued on my lonely walk having put the two glass balls carefully into my haversack. I then came to an empty coastguard look-out hut. This hut was only manned in conditions of very poor visibility. Its close proximity to the rocky coastline served as an advantage to the Coastguard Officer when on duty there, as he could observe as well as hear shipping at close quarters. I proceeded further along and soon reached the Bloody Bridge side of Annalong harbour. I then came across a very picturesque water wheel driving some machinery. I was able to watch it turning but could not see what it was driving in the adjoining premises. I walked on until I passed a built up area and here I emerged onto the main Newcastle to Kilkeel road. I then back tracked for half a mile in the direction of Bloody Bridge, crossing over the road and climbing up into the lower approaches of Mullertown and up to Rourke's Park. Here on the right after leaving the metalled roadway I set off on the grass-like track in the direction of Ballagh Bridge. Because of the elevated position of this track, I had a grand panoramic view over the sea

Ben Crom Reservoir, 1964.

Ben Crom Reservoir, 1962.

with occasional glimpses of the coast road below. On reaching the section of pathway I then walked the well worn descent to Ballagh Bridge. I made use of the rough track to gain access to the main road once more and shortly returned to my L.E. Velocette.

I decided to head for home and as I rode through Newcastle my eyes caught sight of the little clock in the window of a shoe shop on the right hand side of the street. This particular clock was recovered from the wreck of a naval ship which was wrecked on the beach a great many years ago not far from the Slieve Donard Hotel. I headed on then to Dundrum, through Ballynahinch and finally to Belfast after spending a very pleasant day exploring some of the most fascinating parts of County Down and entirely without crowds.

Electric Storm in the Mournes

One day to enable me to spend all day climbing in the Mournes, I left Belfast at 5.00 a.m. to cycle down. I approached the tiny hamlet of Maghera which consisted of about a dozen houses and lay between Bryansford and Dundrum. It was here I took some photographs of a strange cloud formation which hid the Mournes from view. The rest of the sky was clear but I heard faint rumbles as I climbed the steep ascent to the Hare's Gap. I had obtained permission to leave my bicycle at a farm further back. I continued climbing to the top of the ridge on the left above the Hare's Gap. I walked in the direction of the Castles of Commedagh, so called because of their castle turret-like appearance. It was here I heard sounds like something cracking. On lying down in the heather I was just in time to see a little strip of intense blue lightning rushing along the ground until it disappeared. It happened many times always preceded by a little cracking sound. About then there was also the smell of a strange fume-like substance in the ozone. As I experienced this I recalled my Uncle Tommy telling me that he had also witnessed a similar form of lightning rushing along the ground at Frazer Street, Belfast leaving a sulphur-like smell behind it. As on this occasion in the Mournes there was no rain.

I was not concerned for my own safety at this stage and I actually took short walks along the ridge but things started to change dramatically as the cloud base closed ever lower about me. A thicker bar of light came along the surface of the ground emitting showers of sparks and again accompanied by the peculiar smell. My ears were deafened by a terrific bang. I was quite frightened by this outcome of events and after taking some photographs while lying down I decided this was no place to be and ran to get lower down the hillside as quickly as possible.

When I arrived at the farm again the farmer told me he was quite worried about me being up the mountains in such conditions. He said he would never venture up in any kind of storm never mind an electric storm which I had just encountered. I started to cycle back home but as I reached Bryansford I stopped to take more photos of the white belt of cloud which had now spread along the very ridge where I had been some hours before. I set off again for Belfast. There was still no rain but the low rumbles of thunder were still evident in the distance. As the miles drew me further away I stopped several times to take more photos. As I entered Dundrum I stopped again and joined a group of locals who were in a crowd watching the electric storm over the Mournes. They were very interested to hear I had just come from the mountain and wanted to know what it had been like.

Later when I arrived home I developed my film which included photos of the storm. I was disappointed the lightening did not show up in them but I did manage to capture some of the ominous moods of the sky.

Electric storm over the Mournes, 1962.

Chapter 12

FROM MAGGIE'S LEAP TO CLOUGHMORE STONE

Maggie's Leap

Maggie's Leap, a deep gully, is located about a mile further along from Newcastle Harbour in the direction of Annalong. Folklore has it that Maggie was carrying a basket of eggs when chased by a man. To escape from him she jumped the gully and landed safely on the other side without breaking the eggs.

On one occasion in the 1950s I, along with Mike Suchard, who was then the Club's Diving Instructor, decided to explore from the sea the gorge at Maggie's Leap. We were both in our diving suits and spent about an hour here actually swimming right to the back of the gorge landing among the seaweed in a very shallow cave. The atmosphere here with the sound of surging water was quite weird. Mike was not amused when I uncovered the carcass of a sheep. I was quite surprised at the amount of driftwood which found its way into this narrow gorge.

We swam out again into the bright sunlight and at a slow gentle crawl made our way about a hundred yards from the rocks. It was while enjoying this slow swim that by chance on looking up at the almost vertical rocks I saw what looked like a small open doorway on the steep rocky hillside. While Mike was keeping watch from the sea I went ashore and started climbing the rocks. It was impossible for me to spot the door from my vertical position. Meanwhile Mike was treading water and when he saw my plight he started to direct me by hand signals until I at last found the doorway. I felt quite excited as I made my way into the man made chamber which was approximately 6-ft long by 3-ft wide by 4-ft high.

Disappointingly it was bare except for a large coil of rope which was in such poor condition that when I tried to lift it, it started to disintegrate. I signalled to Mike to come up and see for himself. While I was waiting for him to come ashore I examined the doorway and found rusted hinges where a door had been at one time. As there was not enough room for the both of us in the small chamber I made my way straight down to meet Mike and then he went up to have a look. When he came down we discussed this unusual man-made cavity which could only be seen from the sea and wondered for what purpose it had been used.

We made our way down to the water again and both donned our aqua lungs. This time we swam out about 200 yards from the rocks. With a nod we both sank gently to the rocky sea bed almost 40 feet below. This distance out from the coastline the rocky bottom changed to sand. As we were swimming around our attention was drawn to a large boulder which had a sea plant clinging to it. The sea plant stood about 6-ft high with its little antennae at intervals up its stem. The stem was almost transparent and was about two inches in diameter. It made a beautiful sight swaying in the current. After admiring it for a while we then swam close to the bottom. The underwater visibility was superb giving us a wonderful view across the sea bottom with its different types of little creatures going about in their natural habitat. Even though Mike and I must have looked huge to these little sea creatures they seemed to understand we meant them no harm.

As we swam further out in deeper water another change took place on the sea bottom. The seaweed became shorter in length around six inches high compared to around 3 to 6 feet nearer the shore, and instead of being in masses like an underwater forest, it dwindled into clumps usually close to small boulders. This may have been due to the lack of sunlight or oxygen at the greater depth.

Bloody Bridge Youth Hostel

On one occasion I had pre-booked a Saturday night's stay in Bloody Bridge Youth Hostel in the early 1950s. The hostel is situated about a quarter of a mile from Bloody Bridge. A massacre occurred in this vicinity in the 1600s and it is said the river was red with blood and this is how Bloody River and Bloody Bridge were so named. This was to be my first introduction to youth hostelling. I left Belfast at 5.00 a.m. on my bicycle. Although it was quite cold when I started off, I was not long in warming up as I covered the miles. The sky was very clear that morning. Eventually I arrived at the Youth Hostel which was situated some distance up a hillside in the locality of Bloody Bridge. I was booked in by the 'travelling warden' Richard Young who made me, along with the other cyclists, very welcome. This was the first time I met Dickie, as he was affectionately known to his friends and it was to start a lasting friendship with us and our two wives in later years. The term 'travelling warden' meant that because of the hostel's remoteness, it did not warrant a resident warden and it was serviced by a rota of wardens who travelled round different hostels.

The night was very still as all the residents from the hostel sat outside. We were captivated by the spectacle of a very large moon rising over the sea. We watched as the reflection of the moon's rays spread across the calm sea until it met the land several hundred feet below the hostel. The silence was broken by a titter of laughter from Richard who was inside the hostel. As we glanced over we could see him with headphones on listening to a programme on his crystal radio set.

As the night air became very cold we all retired inside the hostel. Later on that night another group of lads came to the hostel looking for unbooked accommodation but they had to be turned away as the hostel was full. They set off to head across the mountains in the darkness to the next hostel in the area of Slieve Naman. We were all amused to see them eating large chunks of solid cold custard as they clambered over the rough ground. Their laughter could be heard for a considerable distance as they dropped down towards the Brandy Path. They seemed not have a care in the world. Dickie told us they might even stay the night in the cave at the Hare's Gap. The next morning, Sunday, we all cleaned up the hostel and dispersed. As I cycled through Dundrum, Dickie caught up with me and accompanied me back to Belfast where he also lived. Although I hostelled later at Cranny Falls and Whitepark Bay, I did not pursue it, preferring camping and the wild outdoors.

Annalong

It was over a period of 10 years while I was a member of a SUB AQUA diving club in the 1950s we spent many weekends diving along the Annalong coast in Co. Down using Bloody Bridge as our base.

Mike Suchard with the author on right holding a sea urchin at Bloody Bridge, 1956.

One of the days Mike Suchard and I were diving in the area and on returning to our base at Bloody Bridge we decided not to use the aqua lungs. Instead we went for a long swim in our rubber suits as far as Annalong harbour. The evening was now calm and we made steady progress by lying on our backs and swimming past familiar parts of the coast which I had known well and walked along. We took advantage of the fact that there was no wind and swam a quarter of a mile offshore.

We had a most unusual view of the Mourne skyline. If it had not been for the houses we would have found the little harbour at Annalong quite difficult to spot against the sloping tree-lined background. On entering the harbour the tide had been fully in and was just on the turn. I guided Mike along to the unusual opening into the small inner harbour where we treaded water while I explained to him the workings of the sluice like device which prevented water from an incoming tide entering the inner basin. This was done by means of two large vertical slots in the stonework on each side of the inner harbour entrance. Large timbers could then be dropped down these slots on top of each other thus sealing it off. Although I never saw this being used I assumed it was to keep the inner basin dry to allow repair work to be carried out on various craft. The device could also be used to retain water in the inner basin after an incoming tide. We only stayed there about half an hour and as we were swimming out again through the entrance, one of the fishermen jokingly shouted to us that we did not need boats with the gear we had on!

The return swim was delightful because the sun was low in the the western sky and the mountains cast long shadows over Annalong. Instead of swimming a considerable distance offshore, we decided to stay within the depth of 15 ft even though this meant we experienced the effects of a slight ground swell in the water. During the swim back to Bloody Bridge the coastline was always changing. Mike and I wondered what it would be like there in an easterly gale. Another time I myself, clad in full diving gear, entered the water at a little beach within walking distance to the left of Annalong Harbour. I did not expect to find anything there other than sand and rocks but my eyes opened wide at the sight of a large almost circular like amphithreatre about 20 ft deep in which quite large fish were swimming. The water was quite calm although the

EXTINCT VOLCANO EXPLORED IN 1950 IN DIVING SUIT

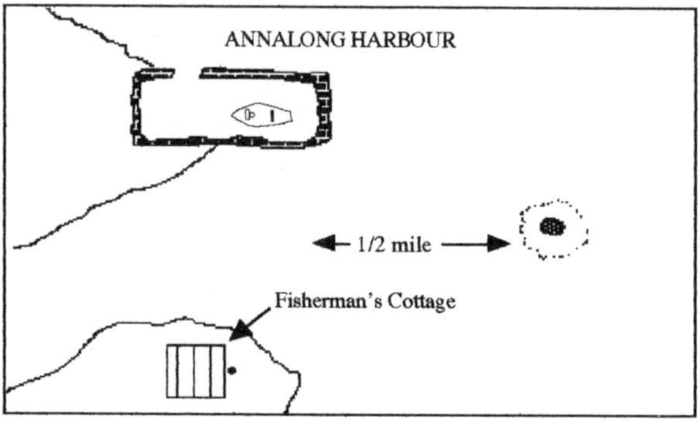

Sketch of extinct volcano at Annalong, 1950.

sea around was choppy. The sides of the inner cavity were quite steep. I swam up one side and out again to the open sea where I found another much larger circular crater. It gave me the impression that a volcano had been formed but later the top had been removed leaving an internal view of the crater covered by the sea. I have brought many friends to dive there over the years to see this spectacle and they have all been quite amazed by it.

Where Bloody Bridge River flows under Bloody Bridge to meet the open sea is a phenomenon which was well known to us divers. I experienced it first in my early days of diving when a group of us approached a certain area where fresh water was flowing from the river out into the sea. Fresh water does not disperse readily into salt water and we had apparently come across an area of this. In fact at this spot the two different waters could be seen with the naked eye. The belt of fresh water had a clearer appearance. As we hit this we immediately began to sink. This experience of sinking was more pronounced due to the lead weight belts we wore. A diver, if he intends to dive in fresh water, will reduce his weight belt by several pounds to counteract the lack of buoyancy. However because we hit this area unexpectedly we had to use our fins more violently to thrust our bodies upwards. We always found this particular area very good for instruction purposes for learner divers. It taught them how to equalise their ear pressure and balance their breathing under these varied conditions

Seaweed or Kelp Industry

One day in the 1950s I cycled along the main coast road from Annalong to Kilkeel. I came to the spot where the road runs very close to the sea and is almost one hundred feet above sea level. Between Ballymartin and Selk Island is an opening in the wall. I went down the very steep steps which led to a sandy beach below which was about 50 yards wide. This particular day the weather was very hot and sultry and I was glad to be wearing shorts. As I walked along the beach the scene which unfolded before me was just like a picture out of the Charles Dickens era. In long lines along the narrow beach were several wooden framework stands about 6-ft high and approximately 160-ft long. A number of ladies were all clad in long dark dresses trailing on the ground. The upper parts of the dresses were covered up to a tight fitting neck. The dresses also had full length sleeves tightened in at the wrists. On their heads the ladies all wore wide brim hats with netting covering their faces. The hats were tied down with scarves. I was completely taken aback by this strange garb which was more reminiscent of an American wagon train dress in the last century except that these kelp ladies were all in black. The several men there were also well protected wearing hats with netting covering their faces and necks similar to that of a bee-keeper. Their trouser legs were tucked into their socks. Both men and women were covered from head to toe. A little industry was in progress here with the men drawing carts of seaweed from a huge pile stacked just above the high tide level. They transported this across to the groups of women who in turn spread it over the long frames to be dried by the hot sun. Other women then took the dried seaweed or kelp across to two other women who were tending an oven like fire. The dry kelp was then roasted on this red flameless fire. Clouds of blinding black smoke arose from the roasting kelp. The smell was so pungent I found myself choking and my eyes began to water severely. Two women with long thin spades gently withdrew the grey white ash which was all that remained of the roasted kelp. This was put aside to cool and then shovelled into bags as fertilizer for distribution.

As I wandered among the racks of kelp, millions of tiny midges descended on me. It got so unbearable I took to my heels and fled. I made my way back to my bicycle and climbed the short vertical steps back up to the road. As I cycled away at speed I could still hear the kelp ladies laughing at my plight. I also knew the reason for their head to foot covering in the middle of a heatwave.

Cloughmore Stone — Rostrevor

This mammoth Cloughmore stone was also known as the 'Rocking Stone'. I first learned about it from my father and visited it a few times with my parents. My father said it was alleged to have moved at times when pushed and that is how it became known as the 'rocking stone' although I must admit I have never ever seen it move. In the early 1950s I set off early one morning by bicycle with my friend Eddie Hunter to Rostrevor.

Our purpose was to see the stone which was situated a quarter of a mile from Rostrevor on the Kilkeel Road and it took us 6/7 hours to cycle down. At that time it entailed a good half mile climb from the roadway up a narrow twisted path. A few yards up this path there was a little wooden cafe in among the trees which sold teas, cakes and ice-cream. There were also a few tables and seats outside. Nailed on one of the tree trunks was a very large ICES sign. We were glad after the hot cycle run to have a large ice-cream cone each before continuing on up the path. Further up we left our bikes locked together off the main track and climbed up the rest of the way. Little did we know we would be involved in a rescue bid at the stone. As we climbed past the tree line the massive stone came into view and as we approached the summit we realised something was wrong when we saw a crowd of people at the base of the stone and heard a lot of shouting. When we got up to it we saw a man clinging precariously by his hands on one side of the stone about 15 to 20 feet from the ground. He had obviously climbed up the most difficult side which was tapered at the bottom and bulged out further up which meant when he got up so far he could not see down below to get a foothold. I had climbed this stone on previous occasions and knew the most accessible side so I started climbing up to the top while Eddie climbed up from below to where the man was hanging on. Eddie was able to assist him in getting a proper foothold while I lowered myself from the top and caught hold of his wrists. With Eddie working from the bottom with his feet and me working from the top with his wrists we managed between us to get the man safely down. He was trembling from fright and exertion and someone in the crowd produced a flask of tea. Eddie and I climbed up the stone ourselves and sat for a while at the top admiring the view. We climbed down again and made our way to the bicycles stopping again at the cafe for a cup of tea. We headed for Rostrevor just to see around before starting again on the long journey home to Belfast.

★ ★ ★ ★ ★

This concludes my memories of exploring around County Down and perhaps will give the reader inspiration in future to TAKE A SECOND LOOK!